LIONCREST
PUBLISHING

Copyright © 2022 John Lincoln

All rights reserved.

Advolution

How to Build a Systematic, Self-Improving, and Future-Proof Digital Marketing Program

ISBN 978-1-5445-3502-9 Hardcover

978-1-5445-3501-2 Paperback

978-1-5445-3500-5 Ebook

JOHN LINCOLN

ADVOLUTION

HOW TO BUILD A SYSTEMATIC, SELF-IMPROVING, AND FUTURE-PROOF DIGITAL MARKETING PROGRAM

CONTENTS

To my wife and two kids.
Thank you for inspiring me
to be better every day.

INTRODUCTION

My friend was struggling.

His company was underwater. He was living paycheck to paycheck, barely able to make ends meet for his family. As the bills piled up, his anxiety grew.

It wasn't that he was a bad businessman. His company had a great product, and they'd been doing reasonably well over the past few years.

The problem was his digital ad agency.

A few months prior, my friend had decided his company needed to grow its market, so he hired an agency to help him. But they didn't help. Almost overnight, his company saw a 50 percent dip in revenue.

Just like that, half of his business was gone.

My friend came to me desperate for answers. If he didn't right the ship soon, his company would be sunk—and his livelihood along with it. At the time, my own company, Ignite Visibility, was still in its infancy. But even in our earliest days, I knew our formula worked. More importantly, I knew it would work for him.

So, we got to work. First, we built out his presence on the big digital channels: Facebook, YouTube, and Google. Then, we built out other digital fundamentals, optimizing his presence for the web and boosting his email marketing capabilities. Finally, we turned to his website, improving the design and boosting his creative output.

Eventually, we maxed out his presence on every available channel. So, we created another website and did the whole process again. Then, we created another website and did the same thing again. And then again.

By this time, not only had he reached the total addressable market for his niche, but he had also moved into other adjacent niches as well.

Nine years later, my friend's business has grown by 30 to 50 percent each year since we began working together. No longer living paycheck to paycheck, my friend now has complete financial freedom, making millions of dollars a year. This is the kind of freedom he dreamed of when he first started his business. And once he was able to build a reliable digital marketing platform, he was able to make that dream a reality.

Our approach was systematic and thorough, and that's the thing: in digital marketing, systematic and thorough wins the day. Regardless of the business size, a systematic approach wins. Unfortunately, far too many businesses—and the ad agencies they hire—fail to understand this. This approach worked for my friend, and over the years, it became clear to me that it would also work for mid- to large enterprise businesses. But I am getting ahead of myself. Let's take a step back.

THE NEXT EVOLUTION OF YOUR DIGITAL MARKETING STRATEGY

If you picked up this book, then, like my friend, you're probably not seeing the results you want with your digital advertising efforts. Maybe you're actively losing money. Maybe you keep running into pesky technical or legal issues. Maybe you're just underwhelmed with your returns and looking for answers.

Whatever the case, it's time to add certainty to your digital marketing strategy. If you're tired of the guesswork and ready to implement a proven framework of success, this book is for you.

Digital marketing has revolutionized the ad game. With so many channels and so many cost-effective options, the barrier to entry has never been lower. Anyone who wants to can advertise online. This is both a blessing and a curse.

While there are some truly excellent digital marketing programs out there, many more are entirely ineffective and rudderless. As my friend learned the hard way, working with inexperienced marketers won't just cost you upfront. It can have a serious negative impact on your bottom line in the long run. Most of these marketers mean well, but they lack the strategies, tactics, and foundational principles to guide your decision-making and build an effective and reliable digital marketing operation.

This isn't just wasteful; it's dangerous. Every day, I see marketers run into problems that they could have avoided:

- They're not legally compliant online.

- They're tied up in YouTube ads when they could be making three times as much money on Google Search Ads.

- They're over-indexed in social media when they should be leveraging their massive database for email marketing and paid media campaigns.

- They're constantly setting up new programs and then abandoning them because they have the wrong strategy or never give the programs enough time to work properly.

What you don't know will cost you. At best, your marketing efforts will be inefficient, and you'll fall short of your goals. At worst, an uninformed approach could leave you open to potentially disastrous legal consequences—or getting kicked out of Google organic search (or another ad network) entirely. Either way, that's no way to run a profitable business.

But while digital marketing may often make those who don't understand it apprehensive, it's also necessary to succeed as a modern brand. More organizations are coming online than ever before. Many of them have seemingly bottomless resources, setting up robust digital marketing programs quickly and effectively.

Here's the good news: building a digital marketing program has never been easier, if you follow the right steps. With a sound strategy and a consistent approach, you can create a reliable, scalable digital marketing operation that will add stability and certainty to your business—and ultimately, to your bottom line.

A PROVEN FRAMEWORK FOR DIGITAL MARKETING MASTERY

The future of the web comes down to two things: who can put the best digital marketing strategy in place and who can convert the most traffic for less.

Whether you're new to the digital marketing space or you're an experienced practitioner looking for a better framework, this book will give you the tools you need to create a world-class digital marketing program. While the tools, practices, and even the laws surrounding digital marketing are constantly changing, I have written this book with one eye on the present and one eye on the future.

The best digital marketers don't just know what to do; they know why they're doing it. The tools and information in this book will give you both. Through my framework, not only will you develop an executive-level knowledge of how to approach digital marketing, but you will also learn how to identify and avoid the most common pitfalls that marketers face today.

My framework isn't theoretical or academic—these practices have been painstakingly pieced together over the course of thousands of different advertising campaigns. Through these experiences, my colleagues and I have developed what we believe is the perfect framework for digital marketing, paid media, and ad strategy.

I first began working in the digital marketing space in 2002 and got serious about it in 2007. I worked in in-house marketing teams, was a director at a publishing company, and then a director at an agency, all while running a variety of online businesses. In 2013, I co-founded Ignite Visibility, now a leader in premier digital marketing solutions. We've worked with some of the biggest brands in the world. Until 2018, I also taught digital marketing at the University of California in San Diego, training the next generation of marketers in some of the exact same approaches you will find here. I stopped teaching there to spend more time doing what I love—working out; spending time with family, friends, and clients; and focusing on my businesses. Turns out, I enjoyed working on the largest and most advanced digital marketing programs, while also serving as CEO at Ignite Visibility, more than teaching.

The scope and range of my work have given me and my talented teammates at Ignite Visibility a unique perspective of the digital marketing world that few others possess. This book draws heavily not only from my wisdom, but also from the contributions of Eythor Westman, Connor Brown, Christian Nicolini, Meghan Parsons, Ryan Cox, and Eric Bodziony. Through our shared perspective and skill set, we can work with any business owner, any entrepreneur, or any friend, and we can help them make more money online. Here, I'm sharing the same formula for success that I used with my friend I mentioned earlier so that you, too, can have the confidence to take your digital marketing efforts to the next level.

Today, I have the honor of working with the largest digital marketing programs in the world—some of which are billion-dollar companies spending hundreds of millions on marketing. I've seen it all, from the start of an effort to full market saturation. But no matter who I work with or how big their marketing budget, my goal has always remained the same: to provide the best strategy that will bring the fastest results for the lowest cost. Overall, I get to help others find greater success in their lives and careers.

This book is an extension of the work I've done for years, both in the San Diego community where I live and internationally as well. In this spirit of service, we've chosen to donate the proceeds from this book to one of my charities, Rady Children's Hospital in San Diego.

There Are No Shortcuts to Success

We're just about ready to get started. But before we do, a few points of clarification.

First, this book is not an exact how-to for running Facebook, YouTube, or Google ads. There are hundreds of courses, blogs, and articles online that can tell you exactly how to do that. (In fact, if you do want to learn specific tactics, take a course at JohnLincoln.Marketing, a website where I add one new marketing course a month. You can also take advanced classes on these tactical items on our YouTube channel or through the Google or Facebook learning center.)

Instead, this book offers a framework for *how* to think about digital marketing. I take a unique approach to multichannel digital marketing and paid media strategy, managing them together for the highest return and the lowest cost, using the best networks online. To achieve this, first we will look at the current trends in the digital marketing world over the next few years based on a unique study that my team and I conducted. Then, we will build up a conceptual framework for how to succeed in that world.

Second, this isn't a book about granular optimization. This book is much more concerned with strategy than with tactics. It's more a book for executive business owners, entrepreneurs, or chief marketing officers (CMOs) than it is for your Facebook ad manager who only works within one platform. (To be fair, this book will help your Facebook ad manager as well, because it will teach them how to be more strategic, formulaic, and systematic—as well as to have a better business sense—but ultimately, this book is meant for understanding the big picture rather than going into the details.)

Third, we did our best to keep this book free from bias. Every platform out there—be it Facebook, Google, or TikTok—wants you to invest the majority of your marketing dollars (if not all of your marketing dollars) on their platform. I don't represent any of these platforms, and I am not incentivized to push you toward one channel or the other. (While my agency charges to run ads for clients, we don't charge more for one network than another.) In this book, we will examine a broad swath of the many channels available, and then I'll give you a framework for choosing those that make the most sense for you and that will generate the maximum return for your brand.

Finally, this book is not a quick-fix solution to digital marketing. Yes, you will get tactics that will boost your bottom line. However, this book is primarily meant to help you adopt a proven formula that aligns with your long-term vision. Rome wasn't built in a day, and your marketing strategy won't be either. One of the biggest misconceptions I see with new marketers entering the digital arena is that they think it will be quick and easy.

It's not.

Digital marketing is hard work. It takes time and effort to build up the necessary expertise. If you think you can learn digital marketing over a weekend, or if you think that you can hire an agency to solve all your problems and build a profitable operation, this isn't the book for you.

Digital marketing is more competitive than it's ever been—and the competition is only growing. A lot of businesses have been in this space for a lot longer than you. They've invested five, ten, or twenty years of their lives into this world, and they're very good at what they do. No matter your industry, you'll be competing against these businesses.

If you're willing to put in the time, this book will give you the foundation to not only succeed but to thrive. I truly believe that there's never been a more exciting time to be in the digital marketing space than right now—and I'm thrilled to give you the tools and strategies you need to achieve online success.

If you're ready, let's get started.

PART 1

THE CURRENT STATE OF PAID MEDIA

CHAPTER 1

UNDERSTANDING
THE BASICS

Before we get into it, I want to make sure you understand certain terms and concepts that I'll be using throughout the book.

Let's spend a minute on this. If you already know these, you can skip ahead.

- **Ad networks.** A network refers to all the different places to advertise that can be accessed through a single location. Ad networks include Google Display Network, Google Search Network, Meta Audience Network, etc.

- **Attribution.** This is the process of associating a metric with a particular advertising platform.

- **Audience.** In the case of digital marketing, an audience is the group of people you advertise to online.

- **Bid strategy.** A bid strategy automatically sets an amount you are willing to pay for an ad result, such as an impression, click, or a conversion.

- **Campaign type.** This is the type of marketing campaign you're running based on your goal.

- **Channel.** These are high-level online traffic categories indicating how people find your site. Common channels are direct, organic, social, email, affiliates, paid search, other advertising, and display.

- **Cookies.** Also known as web cookies, internet cookies, or browser cookies, a cookie is data that's placed on your web browser that allows for certain types of tracking and is used for advertising. Third-party cookies come from a website other than the one you're currently viewing. Third-party cookies are tracking codes that are placed on a web visitor's computer after being generated by another website.

- **Cost per impression (CPM).** Derived from Latin, this term stands for "cost per mille," or cost per thousand impressions. Mille is Latin for thousands.

- **CPC.** This term stands for "cost per click."

- **CRM.** This stands for "customer relationship management." This is a technology for managing all of your customer relationships and interactions online.

- **CTR.** This stands for click-through rate. CTR is the number of clicks that your ad receives divided by the number of times your ad is shown: clicks ÷ impressions = CTR.

- **Data management platform.** According to Oracle, "The data management platform collects, organizes, and activates first-, second-, and third-party audience data from various online, offline, and mobile sources and uses that data to build detailed customer profiles that can be used for advertising and personalized initiatives."[1]

- **First-party data.** Data that you own and have collected. This generally implies you own rights to this data and can utilize it legally. This is also known as 1p data.

- **Funnel.** A funnel encompasses all the different touchpoints you have in your marketing, from where it begins, through the middle, and to the end.

- **Google Tag Manager.** According to Google, "Google Tag Manager is a tag management system (TMS) that allows you to quickly and easily update measurement codes and related code fragments collectively known as tags on your website or mobile app. Once the small segment of Tag Manager code has been added to your project, you can safely and easily deploy analytics and measurement tag configurations from a web-based user interface."

---

1   "What Is Data Management Platform (DMP)?" Oracle, accessed October 6, 2022, https://www.oracle.com/cx/marketing/data-management-platform/what-is-dmp/.

- **Impressions.** This is the metric that quantifies the amount of views a piece of online content receives.

- **Lead scoring.** A method of determining which leads result in the best business outcomes. Typically, a lead is scored on where it came from, the stage of the customer's journey, and the likelihood they will buy. The more resources you direct to areas that result in high lead scores, the more effective your overall campaign.

- **Medium.** While a source is the origin of your traffic, such as a search engine (for example, google) or a domain (example.com), a medium is the general category of the source, for example, organic search (organic), cost-per-click (CPC) paid search, web referral (referral).

- **Programmatic and DSP.** A type of programmatic advertising is DSP, which stands for "demand-side platform." According to Taboola, which is a DSP in programmatic advertising, "A demand-side platform (DSP) is a type of software that advertisers use to automate the process of buying ad inventory from publishers."

- **Publisher.** According to Smartyads.com, a publisher is "the owner of the ad inventory where advertisers can place their ads. The publisher can represent the individual or the company whose aim is to serve the ad impression to the target visitor, providing the traffic to the advertiser who paid for it."

- **ROAS.** This stands for "return on ad spend." As the name implies, ROAS tells you how much money you're earning as a result of the amount you spend on advertising. Here's how to calculate ROAS: divide the total revenue you earned from advertising by the amount you spend on advertising, so ROAS = revenue earned from advertising ÷ advertising expense. For example, if you spend $2,000 on Google Ads and earned $4,000 from people who clicked on those ads, then your ROAS is $4,000 ÷ $2,000 or 2. In accounting terms, that "2" means 200 percent.

- **Source.** A source of traffic. An example source would be Google.

- **Tactic.** In this book, the term "tactic" is used to describe an initiative that supports an overall digital strategy that targets an overall digital marketing goal, for example, brand search, non-brand search, prospecting, retargeting, nurturing, or brand awareness.

- **Targeting.** A marketer is "targeting" when they are using audience preferences, based on either your own data or data made available through an ad network, to pick the people they want to advertise to.

- **Third-party data.** This refers to data from other parties besides yourself that you utilize in your marketing efforts.

- **Tracking.** The process of setting up a system to

collect and connect data. Setting this up usually takes place through a platform like Google Tag Manager or through the code of your own website.

Now that you're all set with some of the important lingo, let's dive into the book!

First, we'll look at the results of a comprehensive industry study to help you understand how to choose the right networks and get the most value for your ad spend.

CHAPTER 2

CHOOSING
THE RIGHT
NETWORKS

A business came to our agency for the first time and was spending around $10 million a month total on its marketing. That's $10 million—a ten, followed by six zeroes. That's a big budget by any standard for marketing. Most marketing teams would kill for a budget that size.

While they had a large budget, they weren't getting the results they were looking for, so they wanted to shift their predominantly offline efforts to online campaigns. It was really interesting to see their marketing mix.

With little experience in digital marketing, and a great deal of historical success advertising offline, their team was spending about 80 percent of that massive budget offline and only 20 percent online—and the money they *were* throwing into digital channels wasn't getting them very far. Unsure of what else to do, they spent the bulk of their digital money—over $1 million a month—in a paid media channel that was not leading to the results they needed.

They were paying millions of dollars on one tactic and couldn't point to any clear outcomes to justify the expense. Given our experience, we could meaningfully improve this program.

Clearly, we had some work to do.

The good news? We had plenty of marketing dollars to work with. The bad news was we had a lot of educating to do and needed internal buy-in, which is often the case in my experience.

Over the next few years, we reoriented their marketing efforts around a vast and changing digital landscape:

- We showed them how to get better results—and more customers—on Google Ads through non-branded ads. We set up a model that showed which leads were new to their brand vs. leads that already had brand awareness.

- We diversified their media channels by adding Facebook, Instagram, TikTok, Google Display, and YouTube to the mix—eventually, we stretched their reach to all the major networks.

- We persuaded them to expand even further into niche programmatic networks.

The bulk of our effort was spent not in making the moves but in convincing our client that these were the right moves to make. We did this by reporting ROAS for each marketing channel each day, week, month, and quarter. Using the data we had, we forecasted results as well. I'll get more into that later.

Eventually, the results of a well-balanced portfolio spoke for themselves. This company that had only allocated 20 percent of their marketing spend to digital was now spending 80 percent—and they eventually began thriving on every major network with best-in-class ads, landing pages, audiences, and more. Their bottom line also improved by over 50 percent.

This client's story is all too familiar. Before they came to us, they were relatively unfamiliar with the digital space, so before getting expert guidance, they simply did whatever they'd heard of that seemed to make the most sense. They didn't have comprehensive knowledge or a cohesive omni-channel strategy. They were constantly jumping in and out of programs.

This approach to digital marketing may have worked once upon a time but not two decades into the twenty-first century. If you want to succeed in the new digital landscape, a haphazard approach won't cut it, especially when you stand to make—or waste—millions of dollars in the effort.

We're in a period of substantial change in the digital space. Those who understand this changing landscape are thriving, but unfortunately, they're few and far between. Most marketers are more like my client: they understand that digital marketing is important to some degree, but they don't understand how their outdated approach is hurting them. They're unaware of the major traps to avoid, where (and how) to run ads effectively, and how to track and measure their impact.

If your program is not where you want it, don't beat yourself up. That's why you're reading this book. But before we get into the *how* of running a successful digital marketing campaign, it's important to understand the current landscape of what you're getting into (or are already involved in). Without that broader framework, even the best tactics can be misapplied. Once you're able to see the big picture, you can then reconsider your own thinking about your digital marketing strategy and adapt accordingly.

In this chapter, we'll explore the current digital marketing landscape—who the biggest players are, who is most trusted, and other common pain points. In the next chapter, we'll expand this conversation to include pressing global and legal issues that may impact your marketing efforts.

A SHIFTING LANDSCAPE

Since roughly 2020, the digital advertising market has shifted tremendously. There are more advertising options than ever before, people spend more time online than ever before, and consumers are more comfortable buying online than ever before. Social commerce and online business inquiries are growing faster than at any other time in history.

As shoppers continue to move online, effectively navigating digital advertising has become increasingly complicated. In the beginning, there was only email marketing. Then search engine optimization (SEO) came along, followed by pay-per-click media (think Google and other similar networks), social media, and more. As a result, the internet now represents a vast ecosystem of advertising opportunities. In this way, managing digital advertising has become akin to managing a full securities portfolio: it's important to understand the broad spectrum of options in order to understand the best place to put your money.

To improve our clients' understanding of that ecosystem, my company, Ignite Visibility, commissioned an industry study to clarify the current state of paid media. We surveyed two hundred marketing professionals in the United States to find: What will marketers be focused on over the next few years? Who are the biggest players? Which platforms do they trust online with their money? Which don't they trust, and why? How confident are they, and what are they the most afraid of? Here is what we discovered.

Who Are the Biggest Players?

According to our survey, here are the platforms where marketers plan to spend their marketing dollars through 2023. We asked each marketer to check a box next to a platform they will be spending on to get these percentages.

1. Facebook Ads (65.5 percent)

2. YouTube Ads (57.2 percent)

3. Google Search Ads (46.8 percent)

4. Instagram Ads (39.4 percent)

5. Google Display Ads (39.4 percent)

6.   Amazon Ads (31.5 percent)

7.   Google Discover Ads (30 percent)

8.   TikTok Ads (28.6 percent)

9.   LinkedIn Ads (28.1 percent)

10.   Twitter Ads (27.6 percent)

11.   Snapchat Ads (17.2 percent)

12.   Pinterest Ads (17.2 percent)

13.   Microsoft Audience Network Ads (14.8 percent)

14.   Bing Ads (12.3 percent)

15.   Niche programmatic solutions (16.9 percent)

16.   Other options (2.5 percent)

But it's not just about the players garnering the most dollars. It's also about trust. Just because you're one of the biggest players on the block, that doesn't mean you're the most trusted. When we asked marketers to identify the network they trust the least, the list shifted dramatically:[2]

1.   TikTok (21.7 percent)

2.   Bing (16.7 percent)

3.   Facebook (14.3 percent)

4.   Google (11.8 percent)

5.   Twitter (10.3 percent)

6.   YouTube (7.9 percent)

---

2 It's worth noting that even though Google owns YouTube, Facebook owns Instagram, and Microsoft owns LinkedIn and Bing (Twitter and Amazon are the only true stand-alones), people differentiate the pairs in their minds and don't consider them to be the same company. Users and marketers don't always think about the corporate structure behind the platforms.

7. LinkedIn (6.9 percent)

8. Instagram (5.4 percent)

9. Amazon (4.9 percent)

That's quite a shift! These results say a lot about marketers' buying behavior. When it comes to their ad buy, marketers often don't take the time to think beyond their return on investment (ROI).

TikTok may be the least trusted network, for instance, but 32.5 percent of advertisers report that it's the one they're "most excited" to test. Facebook may be the biggest player in the ads game, but it's also one of the less trusted networks to advertise on.

To a degree, this makes sense. Marketers want to go where the people are, even if they don't fully trust the channel. But to borrow an old cliché, it's good to look before you leap. Be careful about jumping in on the latest platform before you know what you're getting into. Effective marketing is about more than nabbing customers and generating a strong ROI. It's also about association. This is an important concept. Problems can arise when you choose to advertise with networks whose public perception doesn't align with that of your brand. And when your ad shows up in the wrong place on the wrong network, your brand is only a screenshot away from a call to your favorite PR crisis expert. That is no joke—I've seen it happen.

No one wants to suffer the blowback and PR issues that come with advertising on networks that your target buyers might find problematic. Major platforms like Twitter, Facebook, and YouTube have taken considerable heat in recent years for policies and algorithms that contribute to the spread of political misinformation and—I hesitate to use these words, but they're accurate—racist and extreme content. Now, that is a massive can of worms right there. Companies then have to operate at a disadvantage because internal views do not align with content on the ad platforms and moderation policies. While Twitter, YouTube, and Facebook have since taken more meaningful steps to moderate and filter controversial content, the question still presents itself: how should they moderate content, and should they be moderating it at all?

As a result of the polarity of these conversations, many advertisers have pulled out of specific platforms because their core company values do not align with the ad platforms.

Meanwhile, despite being a Facebook (now Meta) property, Instagram has largely been able to escape the negative perception of its parent company to become one of the most trusted platforms around. Unlike Facebook, Instagram is one of the most curated networks out there, taking strong action around policing content where appropriate. Like Instagram, Twitter has been able to edge out Facebook on the trust scale because of its transparency in its practices—although, like Facebook, it has been hounded by controversies surrounding content moderation.

Finally, this brings us to Google. Google doesn't garner much trust either due to the many privacy concerns surrounding their use of cookies (more on that next chapter), and people feel the company's entire motive is to grow ad revenue. YouTube has similar issues, coupled with concerns about the quality of its content. In particular, its algorithm serves viewers more content based on what they've watched in the past, which can amplify misinformation.

If there is something to be learned from these examples, it's be careful who you associate with. When considering any ad network, examine its public perception and learn what its protocols are in terms of censorship and moderation—not just whether it's a big platform with the potential for a wide reach. Fully vet the platform, and where your ads will show up, before you get engaged, and make sure you have a set of criteria that ensures a platform aligns with your brand before you proceed.

In other words, before you allocate your ad spend on TikTok, take some time to understand why they're such a mistrusted network. Is it because the platform is relatively new? Or, is it because the platform simply has relatively few content controls—allowing highly questionable advertisers to appear right alongside major brands like Samsung?

Just because a platform is hot with a growing number of users and advertisers doesn't mean you should jump on the bandwagon and direct money toward it. Your decision whether to use a platform should align with the platform features, the channel performance, and your brand's values and priorities—not just the latest buzz.

UNDERSTANDING THE MAJOR NETWORKS

In this section, we're going to walk through some of the major places to advertise so you can understand whether these networks would be right for you. I've done my best to give you a simple look at the ad network ecosystem and keep it as basic as possible.

Major Platforms

Four of the major platforms for advertisers to be aware of are Google, Meta (formerly Facebook), Amazon, and Microsoft. Each of these platforms is good for all advertisers. Historically, Amazon has been more valuable to product and e-commerce advertisers. However, more recently we've seen some non-e-commerce appear on this platform as well. This section is meant to provide general guidance. That being said, I've always believed you can get value from just about any platform regardless of business model with enough effort and skill. But some platforms clearly lend themselves to certain business models, products, and services.

Social Ad Platforms

In this section, we look at social ad platforms, some of which are part of major platforms. Our goal is to tell you what each platform is generally best for (with an emphasis on *generally*):

- **TikTok.** Great for brand awareness and consideration, as well as direct-to-consumer (DTC) ads, generally for a younger demographic.

- **LinkedIn.** Generally speaking, LinkedIn is best suited for business-to-business (B2B) purposes.

- **Pinterest.** Ideal for product e-commerce, brand

awareness, consideration, and app installs.

- **Snapchat.** Generally useful for brand awareness, especially for younger demographics, product sales, and, in some cases, services.

- **Twitter.** Generally good for brand awareness, media sites, and app installs.

- **Yelp.** Good for local business.

- **Quora.** Good for service-based businesses.

- **Reddit.** Only good for some niche businesses.

- **Nextdoor.** Good for local businesses and some niche businesses.

Demand-Side Platforms (DSPs)

A demand-side platform (DSP) is a system that allows buyers of digital advertising inventory to manage multiple ad exchanges and data exchange accounts through one interface. When it comes to DSPs, here are the biggest platforms to keep in mind:

- **Amazon DSP.** Good for Amazon sellers, brand awareness, and consideration.

- **Criteo and Adroll.** Great for retargeting and product sales.

- **DV 360.** Ideal for video advertisers for brand awareness and consideration.

- **Media Math, The Trade Desk, and Adobe.** Ideal for expanding beyond paid social and Google Display.

These, and many other platforms, represent other popular DSP options that may be worth looking into.

Native Ad Platforms

Native ad platforms are generally secondary platforms that people get into. These can be good options for some products that don't get approved on normal platforms. For these native ad platforms, Taboola, Outbrain, Yahoo Gemini, Nativo, TripleLift, RevContent, MGID, and PropellerAds are the biggest names to know.

Marketplaces

When you want to sell your products through third-party marketplaces—which are designed specifically for e-commerce—there are three major names you must know: Amazon, Walmart, and Target. However, it doesn't stop there. eBay, Facebook, Etsy, Alibaba, New Egg, Chewy, and many others also offer this ability. Most marketplaces charge a fee to utilize their site. Finally, it's worth noting that some of these are general marketplaces, and others are niche marketplaces. For example, Chewy is a marketplace only for pet products.

Directory Websites

If you're selling a service, you'll want to advertise on a directory website, which is the equivalent of a marketplace for e-commerce. Examples would be Yelp, 1-800-Dentist (a place for dentists to advertise), The Knot Worldwide (a place to advertise wedding services), Healthgrades.com (a place to advertise medical services), and more.

Google Properties (All Advertisers)

Google is the biggest advertising company in the world. According to one statistic, in 2021 they did over $192 billion in ad revenue. So, needless to say, they have many advertising options. Here is a top-level breakdown of each Google property to help you get the best return on your advertising dollar:

- **Google Search.** This is one of the top places to start advertising for all products and services.

- **Google Shopping.** This is the best place for product sales.

- **YouTube Video Ads.** Great for brand awareness and demand generation. It is evolving and is now a common part of the marketing mix for most companies, especially with recent developments in attribution. Choose who you want to see your video ads based on location, interests, and more. Your video will appear before or next to related videos or in search results. Video ads can create a one-to-one communication with potential customers. YouTube offers a Find My Audience tool. With Find My Audience, it's easy to get a deeper understanding of your most valuable customers—their interests, their habits, and what they're planning to purchase.

- **Google Discovery Campaigns.** According to Google, "You can use Discovery campaigns to help reach up to 3 billion customers across Google feeds to achieve your performance goals in Google Ads. Thanks to Google's audience and customer intent signals, this campaign type helps you deliver highly visual, inspiring personalized ad experiences to people who are ready to discover and engage with your brand—all through a single Google Ads campaign."

- **Local Search** Ads. Advertising on Google Maps is a powerful way to attract nearby customers. If you run a local business, ads on Google Maps make it easy for people to get to your location.

- **App Campaigns.** Find the people who will love your app. With App Campaigns, you can promote your iOS or Android app on Google Search, YouTube, Google Play, and more.

- **Local Service Ads.** Local Services Ads help you connect with people who search on Google for the services you offer. Your ads will show up for customers in your area.

Meta Properties (Good for All Advertisers)

Meta properties are good for all advertisers. In fact, most advertisers will have some budgets on Facebook, Instagram, and Messenger, and possibly some secondary budget for Audience Network depending on the maturity of the program. Meta also now offers ads on Oculus Quest. According to Android Central, "VR continues to break records as Meta's Quest 2 headset leads the pack, now eclipsing the 14.8 million units sold mark according to new data provided by the International Data Corporation, or IDC for short. That same report shows that VR sales grew 97 percent in 2021, with Q1 2022 bringing that number up to a whopping 242 percent growth."[3] This shows an emerging and immersive place to run ads.

Naturally, Facebook is the primary place most advertisers flock to, followed by Instagram. Outside of the United States, Messenger is very popular: billions of people use Messenger each month. So, this platform usually has considerable advertising customers in regions where it's heavily utilized. According to Meta, "The messages objective lets you buy ads in Ads Manager or the Ads API with the aim of opening Messenger interactions—making it easier to drive conversations at scale. Businesses of any size can use the messages and objectives to interact more personally with people in order to get leads, increase sales and answer questions."[4]

Microsoft Properties (Good for All Advertisers)

For Microsoft properties, Bing Search, Bing Shopping, and the Microsoft Audience Network are the primary places advertisers go to after Google Search, Google Shopping, and Google Display, respectively. These are proven places to advertise, with new integrations coming into play every day. For example, Microsoft Advertising is the only advertising

---

3 Nicholas Sutrich, "Looks like the Oculus Quest 2 Is Still Selling Better than the Xbox," Android Central, last updated June 7, 2022, https://www.androidcentral.com/gaming/virtual-reality/quest-2-units-sold-spring-2022.

4 "Extend Your Reach and Find More Customers with Messenger Ads," Meta, accessed October 6, 2022, https://www.facebook.com/business/ads/messenger-ads.

platform (other than LinkedIn) that allows you to target potential customers based on their LinkedIn profile information; you can target customers based on their:

- Company, such as Microsoft, Alibaba.com, or KLM Royal Dutch Air Lines.

- Industry, such as finance, broadcast media, or law enforcement.

- Job function, such as sales, accounting, or purchasing.

LinkedIn profile targeting is available for search campaigns, dynamic search ad campaigns, Microsoft Shopping Campaigns, and audience campaigns.

The Future of Google Campaign Types

Both Performance Max and Video Action Campaigns are campaign types that Google rolled out in August 2022. These include exciting new features that I anticipate advertisers will want to invest heavily in over the coming years. Let's briefly explore each campaign type to understand their value to your marketing plan.

PERFORMANCE MAX

According to Evan Trevers at Google, Performance Max is the easiest way for performance advertisers to serve across all Google properties so advertisers can ensure they're not missing valuable customers and maximize their performance with Google Ads. Performance Max is a new campaign type in

Google Ads for advertisers with online sales, lead generation, and offline sales (store visits/omnichannel) marketing objectives. The campaign uses the customer's goals as the primary targeting and brings the best of Google Ads automation into a single campaign type to serve across all Google properties (owned and operated and network) resulting in more online sales, leads, or offline sales for our advertisers. Performance Max campaigns are now the next generation of advertising. Recently, Google upgraded shopping and local campaigns to Performance Max.

PERFORMANCE MAX KEY BENEFITS

- **Drive more conversions via full automation.** Performance Max on average drives 13 percent more conversions at stable ROI via using the latest automated bidding, dynamic creative, targeting, and data-driven measurement technology across all Google Ads channels.

- **Future-proof growth.** Budget unconstrained customers who were unable to efficiently grow were able to spend 10 percent more compared to existing similar campaigns with stable CPA once adding Performance Max to their account. In the future, as new inventory is added to Google Ads, Performance Max will automatically expand.

- **Improved operational efficiency.** Performance Max is fully automated and runs across all channels, freeing up time for you to focus on impactful strategic initiatives such as budget planning, adding more compelling creative assets, optimizing via Recommendations, and analyzing Insights that can improve overall marketing strategy.

VIDEO ACTION CAMPAIGNS

Evan Trevers at Google also describes Video action campaigns as the next generation of TrueView for action, designed to drive lower funnel actions, such as website clicks and conversions. Optimized across multiple formats (in-stream, home feed, watch next, connected TV, GVP, and more coming soon!), Video action delivers improved performance at scale through one campaign that runs and optimizes across all formats with smart bidding (tCPA or Maximize Conversions). In order to run Video action campaigns, Google Ads conversion tracking is a requirement. (Pro tip: you can find Video action campaigns under "Sales, Website Traffic & Leads" marketing objectives in the Google Ads interface.)

VALUE PROPOSITION

- **Scaling to top-converting places across YouTube and its partners.** With Video action campaigns, you can scale across top-converting premium inventories, like the home feed, watch pages, Google video partners, and connected TV—all in one campaign.

- **Reaching more potential customers interested in your business.** Using "custom audiences" and "audience expansion" together, you can reach users who are likely to convert based on their search activity while expanding that portfolio to find other similar users.

- **Incorporating Google's machine learning to optimize and automate the whole process.** With all of these inventory sources under one roof, you can now simply manage one campaign across multiple surfaces. And best of all, smart bidding works seamlessly across them to find you more leads, sales, or web traffic to give you a better ROI.

An Alternative: Niche Ad Platforms and Programmatic DSPs

So where does all this leave digital marketers?

In a world where the biggest players are also the least trusted players, should marketers simply pick the lesser of the evils and advertise with the networks they find least objectionable?

Fortunately, there are other options: niche networks and industry publications. Depending on what you sell and what you're trying to accomplish, the big, top-of-mind players might not matter at all. In fact, in many cases, they don't even represent a good investment.

Outside of the major players, there are myriad other places to advertise. Anyone can create their own ad network; all they need is a platform and a place to deploy the ads, whether they own one website or ten, or form partnerships with a hundred other sites. To run an ad network, in other words, you only need traffic and access to the publications' visitors. For instance, at one point, I had five different websites in a very niche network. The sites collectively received around 100,000 visitors a month, and I was able to sell ads on that network. If I would have wanted to expand that ad network beyond sites that I owned, I could have found more sites in that niche and then paid the owners so I could run my ads on their sites as well.

Niche ad platforms and programmatic DSPs are not only on the rise but often generate better returns than similar campaigns on the major networks. Why? Because the bigger the network, the more poor-quality inventory can sneak in. Examples of niche ad platforms or programmatic DSPs include over-the-top (OTT) networks that stream directly to the internet, as well as options like The Trade Desk. According to The Trade Desk, they focus on "powering the open internet with an independent media buying platform that helps marketers reach more customers through a more relevant ad experience."

Whatever their methods, we have found that niche networks can sometimes generate high conversion rates and a reasonably low cost per acquisition (CPA)—despite serving much smaller audiences. However, such networks rank the lowest among options that marketers are excited to test. As a result, niche networks can generate outsized value in a savvy marketer's media mix. While everyone thinks about running ads on Facebook or YouTube, a strategic media buy with the right niche network could result in spending less money and getting more conversions. (We will cover traffic quality in-depth later in the book, as every conversion is not equal.)

To understand the power of niche advertising, let's look at a few examples.

EXAMPLE 1: INDUSTRY PUBLICATIONS

In my opinion, a "niche network" could still mean a big, traditional name.

Traditional and industry publications like *The New York Times*, *The Washington Post*, and *Forbes* can all count as a form of niche network.

Advertising with these publications is simple. You could go through Microsoft Audience Network, Google Network, or some of the programmatic networks, or you could buy directly from the publication itself. Each publication will have its own way of packaging up its users and delivering them to you. If you go directly to *The New York Times* site, for instance, their network might give you more exclusive inventory than you would get by buying ads through Google or Microsoft.

The right decision depends on your approach, bandwidth, and skill set. Do you have a media buyer who can go directly to the publication, or do you want to use an ad platform to advertise on multiple publications like *Forbes* at once? Or do you want to only target *Forbes*? Whatever your strategy, it usually comes down to the different options for targeting, creative deployment, mixing signals with other areas, your advertising, your own website, and then the final ROAS and cost per conversion—all of which we'll discuss later in the book.

I want to spend one more moment on this *Forbes* example:

- You could advertise just on one page on *Forbes*.

- You could advertise on every page on Forbes.

- You could advertise to every user who goes to ten specific pages on *Forbes* and lives in San Diego, California.

In the last instance, you'd be going after a highly targeted user on a niche network. Would this highly specific user profile convert better than if you went after *all* website visitors on *Forbes* in the United States? I'll let you consider that. Another thing to consider would be whether your targeting was so specific that the total pool became too small to meet your goals. But we will talk more about that later. For now, let's look at another example.

EXAMPLE 2: THE E-COMMERCE PROVIDER

In another instance of a well-deployed niche strategy, an e-commerce provider in Florida who sells furniture could combine niche publications with larger networks.

First, they could opt for direct media buys with the top five biggest furniture publications in Florida, so they could develop relationships with them, and run advertorials with them. Next, the e-commerce provider could set up a landing page to receive all the traffic generated from these niche publications. Using a network cookie or email capture strategy for all the furniture publications, they could capture the information of everyone who visited the landing page. Then, they could run remarketing to them on bigger channels, like Google Display, YouTube, or Facebook.

In other words, if the e-commerce provider captured 10,000 people from the Florida publications, they could subsequently run nurturing ads to those same people through the bigger channels like Google Display, YouTube, and Facebook, allowing them to stay in front of these high-quality prospects until they became customers. I deploy this strategy a lot, and later in the book, I'll share my framework.

Take a moment and consider that example. Think how much more powerful that strategic approach to ads would be opposed to just national Facebook ads. I'm not saying you shouldn't do both. I am saying you *should* do both and see which yields the best return.

EXAMPLE 3: THE MID-TIER PLATFORM

While not quite a niche network, mid-tier platforms like Microsoft Bing offer another alternative. Everyone's heard of Bing, but there has been limited education, marketing, and discussion around the platform, so overall trust in the platform is low. Here, marketers' ignorance may be to their own detriment, and Bing could be a fantastic channel depending on your audience.

To understand what I mean, let's look at the typical Bing user. Consumers who use Bing generally do so because it's the default search engine in their Internet Explorer or Microsoft Edge browser. These users tend to be older and less digitally savvy, so they never bother to switch the default to a different search engine, like Google Chrome. As a result, for any products or services targeting exactly this type of user, Bing can be a goldmine.

According to 99 Firms, 70 percent of Bing audiences in the U.S. were over the age of thirty-five, and over 38 percent of users have an average household income above $100,000.[5] Further, while Google had a total market share of **85.55 per-cent** as of December 2021, Bing still accounted for **over 7** percent of the global search market. (In case you're curious, Yahoo's market share was only 2.85 percent.[6])

———

Let's talk a little bit more about marketing challenges and opportunities.

TECHNICAL CHALLENGES

According to our survey, here are the common technical challenges many digital marketers face in approaching online advertising.

#1: Finding Proper Targeting (24.6 percent)

The most-cited challenge according to our study was find-ing proper targeting: nearly 25 percent of marketers report doing so is their biggest pain point. Networks have created so many different variables for targeting someone that many marketers struggle to select a niche enough audience with a high enough return and enough volume to hit goals. Do you target people whose income is in the top 10 percentile? Ten

5   Ana Gajić, "Bing Statistics," 99 Firms, accessed July 25, 2022, https://99firms.com/blog/bing-statistics/#gref.

6   Statista Research Department, "Worldwide Desktop Market Share of Leading Search Engines from January 2010 to July 2022," Statista, July 27, 2022, https://www.statis-ta.com/statistics/216573/worldwide-market-share-of-search-engines/#:~:text=As%20of%20December%202021%2C%20online,market%20share%20of%2085.55%20percent.

to twenty? Twenty to thirty? Under fifty? Depending on how you target, you may end up with a much smaller group of people, but that smaller pool may be more likely to generate conversions.

And that's just one metric. Outside of targeting by income, marketers can also slice and dice by location, interests, what they are in-market for, keywords, other pages they've viewed, and so on. There are so many different variables that advertisers are understandably confused regarding how to target within a network online.

#2: Determining a Budget (19.2 percent)

The second biggest pain point is determining a budget, which is a challenge because marketers don't have clear criteria for setting CPA goals across the many different networks, especially if they are new to digital ads for the business. Furthermore, everyone wants to grow as much as possible while simultaneously saving money on marketing. These competing aims can put noneducated executives and digital marketing teams at odds, making it extremely difficult to align on an appropriate and effective budget. For this reason, I expect to see many more executives in the future with digital marketing backgrounds.

When the economy is strong, cash is in the bank, and executives or shareholders want to grow aggressively, they'll often give marketers large amounts of money without regard to CPA. However, when times are leaner and leadership wants to focus more on profit, they suddenly become concerned with a dollar-for-dollar return. I've seen it happen time and time again.

My advice is to always have 10 percent of overall company revenue dedicated to marketing and never significantly pull back from or exceed that target, regardless of changing economic circumstances. That approach allows you to tailor your marketing plan to a percentage rather than an absolute number. Without a solid grounding in the data, though, it's common for emotions to rule, causing budgets and goals to shift wildly over time.

To reiterate that point, determine a model and stick to it as you scale. Don't ramp up and down. Say you had a great month and think you can pull back next month. That seems to make sense, but what you don't realize is that if you don't keep scaling, a few months from now you'll be hurting for new business. So I'll say it again: models not emotions.

#3: Determining ROI (15.8 percent)

The third most-cited challenge intertwines with many of the others: determining ROI.

Not all marketers have millions of dollars to throw into digital marketing. We have clients who spend $100,000 a year on marketing and others that spend well over $100,000,000. It all depends on the business size, stage in their maturity and growth strategy.

When you are a new or small business—especially if you're not backed by venture capital—you are much more budget-conscious. As a result, you're much more likely to be focused on generating clear returns. Where should they allocate resources? How do they know when they've maxed out a particular network? As we'll explore in Chapter 5, there are systematic, data-based ways to answer questions like these and more.

#4: Creating Creative for Each Network (14.3 percent)

The fourth biggest pain point is the creative content itself that you will distribute through your various channels. More than 14 percent of marketers identify generating creative content for each network as their biggest pain point. (That actually seemed like a *low* number to me.) It shows that many marketers know just how bad their creative is and how big the opportunity is if they could invest in better creative. Their loss, though, is your competitive advantage.

Every online advertising network now needs creative for their advertising to be effective, and different types of creative work better for different channels. What works on YouTube won't necessarily work on Facebook. What works on TikTok won't necessarily work on Taboola. And so on. The networks know this, and they are always working on making it easier for advertisers. They provide photos and videos, suggest text, and more. That is great for industries that are not competitive—in fact, it's fantastic—but in tough industries, these few options just aren't enough to cut through the noise.

Marketers often underestimate the time and resources required to produce effective, compelling creative content for each platform or network. They do so at their own peril. Cut corners here, and you'll never maximize conversion potential. Running bad creative is the same as throwing your money out the window while driving a car. You need the right offer, the right message, and the right media—and you need to hit the right audience at the right time. Do it right, or don't do it at all.

#5: Validating Network Conversion Data (13.3 percent)

The fifth most-cited challenge is validating network conversion data. Unfortunately, most networks have created their own distinct way of setting up tracking and conversion. Meta conversion data is different from Google, which is different from Taboola, and so on. Most of them are reliant on pixels and final conversion, but the problem is—and also the opportunity in another context—they've set up many other metrics as well. For instance, Meta (Facebook) uses "view through" conversion: if someone sees a Facebook ad, the company counts it as a form of conversion, even if the person only watches part of the ad or stumbled on it by accident and actually converted from a Google ad. (There is one piece of good news: most networks offer easy connections to things like Google Tag Manager, which is a platform that enables tracking codes on websites.)

As a result of the confusion, there are myriad issues with crossovers between channels and with accurate conversion tracking. I don't expect this issue to be resolved over the next few years, but for now it takes a bit of rationalization, the decision to rely on one source of truth or general comfortability with a company-approved model. Marketing departments need to come up with a best way to track for their particular purposes, which for beginners often ends up being last click. As the program gets bigger and bigger, however, they generally shift to a linear conversion—attributing an equal amount of the conversion to each touchpoint—or a position-based conversion, meaning for three touchpoints, 40 percent goes to the first, 30 percent to the second, and 30 percent to the final, last-click conversion.

Validating the conversion data and coming up with accurate data modeling are hugely important. Given the tools now available to marketers and the way the marketing landscape is changing, everyone should move toward value-based bidding, connecting the final sale value directly back to the ad and matching ad targeting and bidding with the power of machine learning. Once you have this, the final step is comprehensive data modeling and visualization.

If Facebook claims an entire conversion based on a particular touchpoint but Google also claims the entire conversion, for example, you need the capability to reconcile the two. The only way to tie all the data together is through one unified analytics platform that looks at all the different channels. Value-based bidding is the answer on the single-platform level, but you still need a unified system to track all the different platforms' data, using a data rationalization model that aligns with your organization's goals, such as linear or last-click if you are on more than one network. The answers to this are usually Google Analytics 4, Tableau, Snowflake, or another data tool.

#6: Setting Up Proper Tracking (12.8 percent)

A quarter of the marketers we surveyed identified their biggest pain point as either setting up proper tracking or validating network conversion data. Setting up proper tracking is undeniably an important skill and often requires a developer. Every network has a different way of doing it, and while most integrated with popular CMS platforms, CRMS and code deployment systems, it gets complicated when tracking the entire user journey across platforms that don't like sharing with each other and who all want to be seen as the most important.

Unfortunately, networks almost always have some inflation on their conversion data for their out-of-the-box tracking solution. To these networks, a conversion is any interaction on their site loosely associated with a conversion on yours.

To put this in context, if your business model is built around lead generation, many of these so-called "conversions" would be useless. They're not even leads; they're just errant data input for a purpose other than conversion. Someone might fill out a form for a different reason than the actual purpose of the conversion (like they want to send you something). Someone might put in a test for an e-commerce sale. Neither wants to buy, but they are creating noise in your channel. For example, on our own website, we get 400 leads a month but 100 of those are people selling us stuff and another 200 are clients we probably don't want to work with.

The only way to have fully accurate information is to set up a conversion that connects a specific ad all the way to a completed sale, which you can do through offline conversion tracking. As I'll explain in greater detail in Chapter 4, offline conversion tracking connects your final qualified sales to the ad and is a phrase recognized by major networks.

Validating from the point-of-sale system all the way back to the conversion data shown in your ad network requires investment, but it's worth it. Through offline conversion tracking, you will have a clear view of where the conversion and the final sale actually came from.

Google, Facebook, and other platforms have developed solutions for this, and other third-party technologies can facilitate this for multiple platforms at once.[7] In the past, all the capabilities had to be designed by our development team, but it is easier now. Google, for example, now offers a feature known as enhanced conversions. If you're not familiar with Enhanced Conversions, here is a description from Google:

> *When a customer completes a conversion on your website, you may receive first-party customer data such as an email address, name, home address, and/ or phone number. This data can be captured in your conversion tracking tags, hashed, sent to Google in its hashed form, and then used to enhance your conversion measurement.[8]*

Put another way, enhanced conversions essentially take your final customer data, tie it back to the ad, and refine it through machine learning within the platform. In addition, you can now set up value-based bidding to refine your advertising targeting based off of what has the highest value in your advertising. For example, through this tool you could run more ads to people who spend $100 versus people who only spend $10.

---

7   George Nguyen, "Google Makes Offline Conversion Tracking Easier with Enhanced Conversions for Leads," Search Engine Land, February 24, 2022, https://searchengineland.com/google-offline-conversion-tracking-easier-with-enhanced-conversions-for-leads-380776.

8   "About Enhanced Conversions," Google Ads Help, accessed July 20, 2022, https://support.google.com/google-ads/answer/9888656?hl=en-GB.

We will get more into this multi-faceted concept in Chapter 5. While it might feel over your head if you are new to marketing, I think the most important thing is to understand the capabilities that exist and not necessarily the specifics of how to use them. As I mentioned, it is better to have a specialist set this up for you. It simply wouldn't be worth your time to learn.

MARKETER CONFIDENCE AND THE MARKETING MIRAGE

Measuring marketer confidence can be a tricky prospect. Past studies typically found that about 50 percent of marketers were confident in their ability to properly manage marketing with the changes occurring in the industry. Most recently, we found that 76 percent of marketers were confident in their ability to manage their digital marketing efforts in the face of the changing advertising landscape of the early 2020s. As the Covid-19 pandemic pushed more marketers online, marketer confidence in their ability to handle the nuances of digital advertising actually grew.

In my opinion, this marketer confidence may be at least somewhat misplaced. Since 2020, so much money has flowed into the US economy through the Payroll Protection Program, employee retention credits, and inexpensive loans at historically low interest rates that many marketers have enjoyed massively expanded budgets to absorb the higher cost per customer acquisition. Also, people bought more stuff between 2020 and 2022. We can see this trend clearly manifesting in the rise and fall of Google, Apple, Shopify, and Peloton stock during this period.

That dynamic will change in the future, however, as the landscape gets more competitive and continues to tighten, money becomes less available, the economy evolves, and people buy less stuff. We are already seeing this happen now, and a tech and advertising bubble correction has occurred.

Now that more marketers have moved online and marketers as a whole are feeling more confident, there are two key takeaways:

1. The digital space is becoming more competitive. Suddenly, it's no longer about who can get online the fastest, but who can be the most effective once they're there.

2. High marketer confidence has resulted in more investment in digital channels. But this marketing confidence is sure to wane, as budgets get smaller and more performance-focused. For the record, I am not less confident. I am saying that newbies who rode the wave of deep pockets and excessive consumer demand will face a different reality than they have known.

Knowing this, it is imperative that, as a marketer, you have the strategic fundamentals in place that we cover later in this book. The most successful marketers aren't necessarily the ones who outspend their competition to make the biggest splash. They're the ones who have a specific, strategic, curated, data-based approach to their strategy, digital marketing, ad spend, brand growth, and growth in different channels.

PUTTING IT ALL TOGETHER

Overall, our survey reflects a chaotic reality—one in which marketers often find themselves willing to spend significant advertising dollars on platforms they neither trust nor understand. If you can learn to cut through the confusion and understand where your focus should really be, you'll win as this massive shift in digital unfolds over the next five years.

It comes down to running ads based on the customer who produces the biggest return, powering future ads with machine learning, investing in (and testing) creative, and matching the marketing needs to targeted business growth. All of which is impossible without proper tracking and data visualization.

As I'll explain, the future may look quite different from the present, specifically because the long-used tracking tool of cookies is going away on some level. Eighty-three percent of marketers surveyed reported they weren't concerned about this impending change, and almost 88 percent think alternatives—which we'll cover in more detail—will be as effective as or more effective than current methods. Clearly, though, succeeding in the emerging landscape requires keeping up with the changes. Furthermore, 69 percent of marketers plan to increase their overall budget through 2023. However, this to me again shows irrationality, as I do not believe they fully understand the economics of the cash they have for ads.

While they plan to spend more, despite possibly shrinking funds, there is a misconception on a few things. Let's start with testing. More than half of marketers determine the effectiveness of a new network after testing for only a month or less, and many miss out on the benefits of an iterative testing and refinement process over longer time horizons, an approach I'll outline in greater detail later in the book.

As the survey shows, and as our own experience has borne out, the best strategic approach is one that coordinates the myriad digital options and leverages data in different ways to get the biggest returns. It's not enough to dump all your money with the biggest players and expect to capture your share of the market.

In fact, doing so could be hazardous to your long-term goals. The big players continue to make advertising on their platforms easier with a goal that it is easier for you to spend money and you become dependent on their platform. If they had it their way, with a click of a button they would run your ads, create your creative, create your landing pages, store your data, and provide your analytics. We will see platforms work to make this happen. They want you to become so dependent on them that you don't run ads anywhere else. They don't ever want you to leave their ecosystem. That is how they make more money from you as their customer.

In the following chapters, I'll teach you how to avoid this trap. Don't lock yourself into any one platform. Give the platforms the data they need to run the most successful ad campaign, but keep the rest for yourself. You never know when another channel will completely eclipse Meta or any other platform and people will start spending less time there. Build your own ecosystems, don't over-rely on any one platform, and make sure you're always diversifying.

ACTION ITEMS

Before you get onto any platform, no matter the potential return or how cool you think it might be, ask the following questions:

- What are the network's policies?
- How does the network serve content?
- Who creates the network's content?
- What safeguards are in place so you don't show up next to content that you don't want to be associated with?
- Is the content really good for the brand?
- Does the content align with your brand standards?

CHAPTER 3

NAVIGATING THE LEGAL AND ETHICAL CHALLENGES OF THE MODERN WEB

Do you know what Germany's laws are like regarding collecting cookies and data?

Do you know Norway's policies on sharing touched-up photos?

Did you know that—no matter where you live—if your website is accessible in other parts of the world, then you're potentially subject to the jurisdiction and laws of countries like Germany and Norway, not to mention the EU or even on the state or Federal level in the United States?

When it comes to digital marketing, what you don't know *will* hurt you. Internet law has undergone massive changes since 2015, and even more dramatic changes are still on the horizon. These laws are being enacted on the state, national, and international levels—and they have the potential to dramatically reshape how you do business online. I saw this trend start to pick up steam in 2017 while I was speaking at Web Summit in Portugal. At that time, the EU had just started imposing web regulations. I knew the Wild West days of the internet were coming to an end. Trust me, it will only get more regulated from here. Internet law will be one of the emerging fields of the future.

And yet, millions of websites all over the world aren't in compliance with these laws. Often, these sites are run by businesses so small that government bodies have little reason to go after them, and in some cases, the governing bodies do not have regulations on businesses below a certain revenue or employee size. They just do not have the bandwidth to enforce policies across the entire web. Still, the fact remains: ignore the law, and you could find yourself in legal trouble at any time.

Ask yourself right now: Does your company have clearly written policies and practices surrounding privacy and data collection? How about website accessibility? Do you share the right disclosures on your site that notify visitors that you're using cookies (or any of their other information) and give them a chance to opt out? Do you even know what the third-party plugins and features on your site track? How about your content management systems? Does it sell data?

If the answer is, "Jeez, John, I really don't know," then this chapter is for you. In the following sections, we'll explore some of the biggest legal and ethical questions facing marketers today—and what they can do about it.

Before we dive in, a big, big disclaimer: I'm not an attorney, and none of this discussion should be confused as legal advice. It is not legal advice. I am merely surfacing this information, just as I do with our clients, to bring to your marketing department and legal team to verify the best course of action. So again, this is not legal advice—this is information. That being said, and perhaps the main reason I knew I had to bring this up in a book, I seem to know more about this stuff than many of the lawyers I run into in the field. They typically only get involved when things go wrong. I want to give you this information now so you can get them involved before that.

THE ELEPHANTS IN THE ROOM

Since 2015, arguably the biggest shakeups in the digital marketing space have come through the introduction, or updates to, three high-profile laws governing how marketers collect and use user data. They are known as the Americans with Disabilities Act (ADA), the General Data Protection Act (GDPR), and the California Consumer Privacy Act (CCPA). There are more, but let's start with these and look at each one-by-one.

The Americans with Disabilities Act

The ADA is a federal civil rights regulation, enforced by the U.S. Department of Justice and designed to protect those with disabilities from discrimination. Although the ADA has been around since 1990 and originally did not apply to the internet, it now does. Lawsuits and settlements are common when websites are not ADA-compliant.

The best practices for a website fall under a few areas:

- Focus accommodations to help users navigate your site with a keyboard rather than a mouse, which is critical for motor and cognitive impairments.

- Semantics accommodations to ensure your site is compatible with assistive technology for visual and auditory disabilities.

- Styling accommodations or visual design choices to make your interface as flexible and as usable as possible.

This is not a comprehensive list or legal advice on ADA. My recommendation is to learn more at ada.gov. Also, there are potential shortcuts to some elements of compliance by using tools like accessibe.com.

The General Data Protection Act

The GDPR went into effect in the European Union on May 25, 2018, right after I saw it coming while I was in Portugal. European policymakers wanted to reshape how companies handle and protect individual data and privacy. The GDPR mandates consent to data collection and use and sets out new standards for data breach notifications as well as penalties of up to $20 million for lack of compliance. Under this law, you must disclose data breaches.

The GDPR also contains a "right to be forgotten" clause, which allows users to completely remove their data from any given database, anytime they want. While the GDPR focuses on updating and standardizing existing privacy regulations, it also creates a clear, rigid set of standards that companies are required to adhere to. GDPR compliance isn't mandatory in the US, but if your website collects, controls, or processes data of individuals located in the E.U., then compliance is mandatory because of the globalization of digital platforms.

Even if your business strictly operates in the U.S., privacy standards similar to GDPR are starting to show up on the state level—as well as in other countries like Canada, which recently passed the Canadian Consumer Privacy Protection Act. According to the Commissioner of Canada,

> *Bill C-11, which enacts the Consumer Privacy Protection Act (CPPA) and the Personal Information and Data Protection Tribunal Act (PIDPTA), is an important and concrete step toward privacy law reform in Canada. Arising from the 2019 Digital Charter, and following years of Parliamentary studies, Bill C-11 represents a serious effort to realize the reform that virtually all—from Parliamentarians, to industry, privacy advocates, and everyday Canadians—have recognized is badly needed.*

> *The Bill completely rewrites that law and seeks to*

address several of the privacy concerns that arise in a modern digital economy. It promises more control for individuals, much heavier penalties for organizations that violate privacy, while offering companies a legal environment in which they can innovate and prosper.[9]

Since the U.S. often follows Europe and Canada's lead on consumer-protection issues, we should all take note of the GDPR and new bills forming in Canada, and probably just follow the policies proactively. Better to be a little ahead of the game than to find yourself noncompliant and behind the eight ball down the road.

The California Consumer Privacy Act

The CCPA, which went into effect January 1, 2020, has similar requirements to the GDPR. While the CCPA is designed specifically for California, other states have begun to consider it as a template for their own laws. If you're setting up a new site anyway, it's better in the long run to make sure you're compliant. Make no mistake, this burden falls on you if you are running the website.

OTHER REGULATIONS

Every industry also has specific regulations to take into account. Finance, healthcare, pharmaceuticals, and some

9   To learn more, see: "Submission of the Office of the Privacy Commissioner of Canada on Bill C-11, the *Digital Charter Implementation Act*, 2020," Office of the Privacy Commissioner of Canada, May 2021, https://www.priv.gc.ca/en/opc-actions-and-decisions/submissions-to-consultations/sub_ethi_c11_2105/.

products such as alcohol, firearms, and CBD fall under strict scrutiny by the various legal bodies, such as the FDA, FTC, and FCC, and more, for advertising and marketing. Further, Google Ads prohibits the use of personalization and remarketing for prescription drugs, alcohol, and products that refer to financial hardship. There is a big list of things you cannot do on each ad network. Know your industry.

THE BOTTOM LINE

If your business fails to comply with any applicable laws, you face potentially significant legal repercussions, such as under the ADA, GDPR, and CCPA. Some law firms actively seek out sites that are not ADA compliant and threaten them with litigation. In 2019, for instance, a blind man successfully sued Domino's Pizza in federal court because its website was not compliant with screen-reader technology. This is not only happening to high-profile companies; I personally know at least five small businesses that have been fined.

If you're blissfully unaware of the laws outside your state, federal or global laws could come back to bite you. Wherever your website is available, you're potentially liable. Sure, Domino's is a bigger target than a small, local donut shop, but there are many businesses between those two extremes that offer services to people accessing their site from across the country and around the world. To avoid legal consequences, the best thing to do is to comply with existing laws.

Every business should have a data-collection strategy based on the laws of the state and country in which they operate. Do not ignore privacy laws. Make sure your opt-ins are in order. Bring this information to your legal team as you consider how these issues apply to your particular situation and which regulations apply. This is such an easy problem to avoid, and yet far too many companies I know are getting ensnared in legal challenges simply because they were unaware of how different laws might affect them.

ENTERING A COOKIELESS WORLD

While many of the laws I just described may come as a shock, they shouldn't. The truth is, various companies and browsers, from DuckDuckGo to Firefox, had already taken a firm stance against tracking website visitors independently of these laws. These moves, combined with the implementation of new laws, have created a kind of revolt. Consumers increasingly resist being tracked online, and providers have been moving away from cookies for quite some time.

Third-party cookies have a long and controversial history. Here's the short version: people were being tracked without being aware that companies were gathering and selling their data. While certain browsers have allowed that kind of tracking, others (like Firefox) have not. More recently, due in part to public outcry, in part to the laws we discussed in the previous section, and in part due to the rise of better, more ethical alternatives, cookies have begun their slow march to being sunsetted. As users continue to value and emphasize privacy in their web experience, marketers can no longer rely on the data generated by cookies. We are indeed starting the journey toward a cookieless world.

BIG TECH MAKES BIG CHANGES

Where once it was just companies like Firefox, now Google has taken a stance on cookies as well. The world's largest search engine now believes that not only is the practice no longer sustainable but that it also infringes on people's right to privacy; people shouldn't have to accept being tracked across the web in order to get the benefit of relevant advertising—and advertisers shouldn't need to track individual consumers across the web to get the performance benefits of digital marketing.

In 2019, Google announced it would begin phasing out cookies in January 2020 and stop using cookies in Chrome entirely by 2022. In June 2021, however, Google delayed blocking third-party cookies by an extra year to 2023.[10] Now it has been delayed again to 2024. For now, Google has new privacy restrictions, but it's unclear how they will entirely get rid of cookies.[11] So, I expect cookies to survive in some form past this deadline, but the question is, for how long?

Google isn't the only tech giant that has recently become a more public champion of user privacy, however. Beginning with their iOS 14 update, Apple has given all users the option of opting into or out of tracking. Unsurprisingly, most users have chosen to opt out instead of opt in.

---

10   Richard Lawler, "Google Delays Blocking Third-Party Cookies Again, Now Targeting Late 2024," The Verge, July 27, 2022, https://www.theverge.com/2022/7/27/23280905/google-chrome-cookies-privacy-sandbox-advertising.

11   Jessica Bursztynsky, "Google Plans Privacy Change Similar to Apple's, Which Wiped $230 Billion of Facebook's Market Cap," CNBC, February 16, 2022, https://www.cnbc.com/2022/02/16/google-plans-android-privacy-change-similar-to-apples.html.

This move has sparked a war between Apple and Facebook, as it has effectively cut off the social media giant from collecting data from Apple users. As of this writing, only about 14 percent of Apple users have opted into tracking.[12]

Part of the animosity is due to strikingly different views of privacy and data. Apple believes that users should have a clearly delineated choice, while Facebook says cookies help provide, protect, and improve Facebook products in order to personalize content, deliver targeted ads, and provide a safer experience.

However, there is almost certainly a strategic component to the move as well. Apple is rumored to be building its own ad network and search engine to run natively on its operating systems to replace the deal it currently has with Google. In order to entice users into that ecosystem, it's only natural that they would look for ways to shut out Facebook. Really, we already know this is true. Apple has its own ecosystem in more ways than one, so we can expect them to build out the social aspects even more and eventually also add a search engine.

When we consider all of this, two things are certain: (1) things are getting more complex, and (2) platforms are sharing less data with each other. Our survey found that 41 percent of marketers cite tracking users across the web as one of their biggest challenges moving forward.

---

12   Kif Leswing, "Apple's Ad Privacy Change Impact Shows the Power It Wields over Other Industries," CNBC, November 13, 2021, https://www.cnbc.com/2021/11/13/apples-privacy-changes-show-the-power-it-holds-over-other-industries.html.

EMERGING ALTERNATIVES

The solution to capturing data in the new cookieless web may not be as complicated or as confusing as many marketers think. In fact, many proven solutions are already out there.

- **Focus on creative.** Many companies are learning to rely less on targeting abilities and more on how great their creative ads are. Good creative with great offers will always appeal more to a mass market. You may not be able to target and track your audience, but you can still draw them in with valuable content.

- **Build your database.** Good marketing teams already know the value of a robust CRM and database to capture their own first-party data.

- **Build your email list.** Many businesses have treated email marketing as boring and outdated, but it has remained quite resilient over the past couple decades. Our email department has more than doubled over the last year as we shifted away from cookies and tracking data. Many other companies have followed suit. Recent data shows a huge increase in email marketing, which allows marketers a chance not only to get the best prospect on their list, but to reach out to them directly with offers and discounts.

- **Focus on first-party data or optional, volunteered information.** Even if you didn't have your cookied third-party data, how could you still run the business from a marketing perspective? Set up a value exchange with your prospects so you can capture their first-party data. For example, "Enter your email address for 10 percent off."

- **Embrace contextual targeting.** Contextual targeting involves behavioral targeting of segment audiences based on the content they are browsing on your site. For example, say you have ten different subjects that you cover on your website, each mapped to micro-conversions for email captures and downloads. If you're a bicycle company, your site might have one section about mountain bikes, another about the best mountain bike tires, and another about the best places to mountain bike. In this case, you can offer a guide to the best mountain bikes for that year, a guide for the best tires for that year, and a guide for people to mountain bike as a download. When they download it, you could capture their info, add them to an audience, set up email automation and ads, and nurture them until you make the first sale. After that sale is complete, you could keep them on the journey.

Considering all these options in as a whole, you may see a pattern emerge: to adjust to a cookieless web, we must prioritize "old-school" approaches like customer relationships, customer loyalty, and value exchange. Essentially, make sure you're collecting data the *right* way. Examine your CRM system and ensure you're using all the features and capabilities you can.

And above all, get creative. Instead of one call to action, consider twenty different offers that are each tied to specific content. You can also use technology to increase personalization even further. For example, you could insert a dynamic keyword into a call to action on every page and then map it to an offer. If someone searches for "best bikes" on Google, for instance, you could put an offer on a page that says "buy the best bike now." This kind of customization makes a big difference. By implementing features and solutions that allow for real-time personalization, many marketers are discovering that they never needed cookies to begin with.

TIME TO ADJUST

In the next chapters, we'll explore a promising development in this new cookieless landscape called value-based bidding. But whether you adopt this approach or one of the other alternatives discussed in this chapter, here's the bottom line: start testing alternatives now.

Consider allocating 10 or 20 percent of your budget to those tests. Focus on first-party data collection, amazing ad creative, and valuable services. Practice contextual targeting and CMS auditing. When you spend even a little bit of time on conversion rate optimization, you'll start seeing a clearer path to better sales. Keep testing and keep trying new things. In the meantime, keep doing what works—better creative, better engagement, and better offers.

ACTION ITEMS

For every country in which you operate, it's important to ensure compliance. Laws also vary considerably. For instance, Germany has strict rules across the board, while Norway has specific policies for disclosing whether a photo has been retouched.

- Create a checklist for your industry on the state, federal, and international levels for every country where you operate to ensure compliance.

- Create a data-collection strategy based on the laws of the state and country in which you operate.

- Get your opt-ins in order. Using one call to action across your entire site is much less effective than calls to actions that are specific to content.

- Examine your CRM system and ensure you're using all the features and capabilities you can.

PART 2

HOW TO BUILD A WORLD-CLASS DIGITAL MARKETING PROGRAM

CHAPTER 4

SETTING UP A DIGITAL MARKETING FOUNDATION

A well-known business-to-consumer (B2C) company's brand had become tired. For years, they'd been pushing the same creative ads. They were getting good results, but they wanted exceptional results, and they wanted us to help.

First, we sat down with the various stakeholders both on their marketing team and within the rest of their company, and began reviewing important data:

- Who is the customer?

- What are their pain points?

- What do they like and not like about our client's current service?

After a deep examination of this client's customers over a two-day period (credit to Google as well, who also collaborated with us on this process), we emerged with specific customer pain points, state-level market analysis, brand sentiment analysis, category analysis, and a strategic plan to address these. With the overall strategy, messaging, targeting, and product differentiation defined, it was time to get tactical.

First, we made landing pages and set up email sequences that aligned with those pain points.

Next, we looked at the company's current online assets, including their website and all their advertising channels. No stone was left unturned. With every entry point to their online conversion process, we asked if that page aligned with the strategy, messaging, targeting, and differentiation (both on mobile and desktop). We also ensured the pages followed conversion rate optimization best practices. From there, we set up tracking around each goal as a both micro-conversion and then a macro-conversion.

With everything in place, we then set up a way for the company to monitor its progress. First, we built a dashboard that would allow them to see their conversions in real-time. Then, we worked with the client to set up a report that would allow us to get emails for the entire group, six times a day, showing how they were pacing relative to the goal for that day, overall for the year, and within each channel. Every couple of hours, everyone would receive an email directly tied to the dashboard data, which would later feed into weekly recaps, and ultimately monthly and quarterly reviews.

This program clarity allowed the company to fully control the levels of their paid media and overall digital marketing results. We saw conversions increase from 10 percent to 20 percent to 50 percent over the next four months as we carefully analyzed and tweaked the program. But the best was yet to come. Based on the previous year, we mapped out hot sales seasons and slow seasons, and then built a model based on past data that allowed for unheard-of returns for the company. More on that later.

Their story shows what a well-planned digital marketing campaign can look like from end to end. While many marketers are eager to dive in and start making tactical moves, it's important to have the measurement and strategic basics in place first. In this chapter, we'll take a close look at the key strategic components of a successful digital marketing campaign.

THE VIEW FROM THE C-SUITE

What does it look like to drive a digital marketing program in a landscape that's constantly changing?

In the big picture, the process is relatively straightforward:

- Develop a high-level understanding of the needs

of both your business and your customer, and then match your digital marketing objectives to meet those needs.

- Start small—with just one to three advertising channels. Eventually, depending on the size of your business and the maturity of your program, your reach could grow. For instance, if you were a large, billion-dollar corporation, and your ad spend included offline channels such as billboards, radio, TV, and sports, you could reach up to twenty-five or even fifty different channels. We will talk more about this later.

- Understand your conversions—where they came from, and how much they cost.

- Regularly produce forecasts for the next day, week, month, and quarter. This will allow your marketing team to recommend the appropriate ad spend and project an accurate return that matches the specific business needs at that moment. Not all programs need this level of detail, but all will benefit from it.

- Always be testing. Set aside at least 10 percent of your budget to run new tests on a quarterly basis and look for the best returns.

From a big-picture view, the process is relatively easy to understand. However, to execute on that framework, it's important to understand the world in which you're operating and how that may impact your approach moving forward.

Shifting gears, it's also important for executives to understand digital marketing not only for your KPIs but also to avoid legal liability. The biggest change brands saw and will continue to see in the early 2020s will involve tracking and targeting audiences. Because of regulations like the ADA, GDPR, and CCPA (see Chapter 3), brands will no longer have the targeting abilities they once had.

At a fundamental level, the best way to drive conversions hasn't changed: get someone into your system, run a great ad, and make a great offer. However, over the next several years, marketers will have an exciting new tool at their disposal called value-based bidding. Through value-based bidding, marketers can connect their final sale and revenue all the way back to the marketing media—allowing them to see who actually converted, for how much, and from where. Using that information, over time, brands can run more ads targeted to similar buyer profiles and continue to optimize ad performance. (For a full discussion of value-based bidding, see Chapter 5).

As the world becomes increasingly cookie- and tracking-free, marketers have also begun putting greater emphasis on *contextual targeting*. In contextual targeting, it's not just what the ad is, but *where* it's being run. With cookies and tracking, the relationship between the content and the ad was relatively loose. It didn't matter what blog, article, social media post, or video a person was consuming. As long as the user was being tracked across sites, and as long as these sites were part of an ad network with these capabilities, they were served content relevant to their known interests. Contextual targeting marries the ad to the content. If you want to run an ad geared toward people who want to buy a bike, for instance, the best place to run that ad is on content about bicycles or to someone who has converted before.

Through a practice known as enhanced conversions, you can then use the data generated by someone who has already converted to refine future advertising. According to Google,

> *Enhanced conversions is a feature that can improve the accuracy of your conversion measurement and unlock more powerful bidding. It supplements your existing conversion tags by sending hashed first-party conversion data from your website to Google in a privacy-safe way. The feature uses a secure one-way hashing algorithm called SHA256 on your first-party customer data, such as email addresses, before sending to Google.[13]*

Through enhanced conversions, conversion-based smart bidding, and eventually value-based bidding (and potentially contextual targeting), marketers have the ability to get ahead of the cookie game (see Chapter 3).

Of course, value-based bidding, enhanced conversions, smart bidding, and contextual targeting don't matter much if the end experience is bad. Lifetime customer value is more important than ever. According to Wikipedia, "In marketing, customer lifetime value (CLV or often CLTV), lifetime customer value (LCV), or life-time value (LTV), is a prognostication of the net profit contributed to the whole future relationship with a customer."[14] To achieve that net profit, prioritizing customer relationships is key. Tracking that relationship from a monetary perspective—and then optimizing it—can result in the best returns for your business. Effective

---

13   "About Enhanced Conversions."

14   Wikipedia, s.v. "Customer Lifetime Value," last updated May 13, 2022, https://en.wikipedia.org/wiki/Customer_lifetime_value.

marketing leaders must double down on identifying their best customers and finding ways to maximize their value using first-party data. [15]

DETERMINE YOUR GOALS AND PRIORITIES

Effective digital marketing starts with your overall business goals. In this section, we'll walk through the important high-level questions you must answer before building out your digital marketing operation.

Identify Your Core Business Goals

First, it's important to know what you want not for your marketing operation, but for your overall business. If you want to grow 30 percent per year, for instance, how can you reverse-engineer your processes in order to meet that goal?

Example questions to ask yourself here include:

- How many products do you need to produce?

- How many people do you need?

- How much do you need to expand your operation?

- What's the production timeline?

I cannot tell you how many people want to hire us for a marketing tactic. They think they want to do email marketing, rank number one in Google, or get better click-through rates (CTRs) on their Facebook ads. Then, when I ask them what

---

15   Throughout the rest of this book, I'll use the term customer LTV for this concept.

products they want to sell and how many, they have no idea! Or maybe they don't even have enough products in stock to make the effort worth the time. Long story short, make a business plan and a marketing plan *before* you set out to build out your digital marketing campaign.

Identify Your Marketing Goals

Once you understand your business goals, you can start to map out your own digital marketing program. Here are some questions to ask:

- How much are competitors spending, and on which channels?

- How much am I spending, and on which channels?

- What's my ROAS, my cost per sale, and your customer lifetime value (LTV) for each channel? Do I have the tracking in place to see all this?

- Which channels have we been completely avoiding, intentionally or unintentionally?

Before branching out into a new platform (or site), also ask yourself the following questions:

- How much can I expand my current channels? (I'll help you answer this later with a model.)

- How well does this new platform index against my target audience? In other words, how much of my target audience is there, how much overlap and audience does the new potential platform have relative to the current platform I'm targeting?

- How many of the people on the new site are also on the site that I'm targeting now? Does it give me access to more people or the same people?

- Will I be hitting the same person twice by using this new platform?

- How effective are the new platform/site's targeting capabilities?

- How well does this new platform facilitate conversion actions? (Some platforms don't convert as quickly as Google Search might, such as "Stories" on Instagram, TikTok ads, and Snapchat.)

- Is there any data to suggest advertisers in my vertical are succeeding on this platform? In other words, am I seeing other advertisers on it? (Using tools like Pathmatics, you can see where others are advertising on the web.)

- Is there untapped impression share within my existing platforms that may generate similar performance in terms of impression share? Can I expand the amount of impressions to get 50, 60, or even 90 percent impression share? Can I expand the audiences, and are there more campaign types and targeting audiences within my core platform?

The reason to consider that last point is that with each additional platform you add, you have another to maintain. That means you must launch new ads, monitor more platforms, and likely incur additional costs. Similar to running two websites, this may be worth your time, but, sometimes, you'll find more results by spending more on the platform you're already on.

Finally, one last question to ask yourself:

- Are there measurement, creative, and CRO options that might generate better returns on my current investment before I move to another platform?

Again, the idea here is to make sure you're getting as much as you can from your current platform before you move onto another one—while also keeping a diversified portfolio.

By determining how you stack up against both your competitors and yourself, you can then refine your marketing mix to match those benchmarks and exceed them. All these different sites offer tools—Google offers Performance Planner, and Facebook offers Inventory Insights—to help you understand how much you can get out of your current platform.

Create Your Data Management Plan

Lastly, you'll want to determine a plan for collecting and utilizing data. The big goal here is simple: with every click from every prospective customer, make sure that you're collecting their data through a legal method and that you disclose how you will use that data to them. The more data you collect, the more you build your database—and the less it will cost you to convert new customers and generate more sales over time. Grow your first-party data. Become a master!

The key to good data management isn't just what you track, but how you use it. With good data management, you can:

- Report on your customers with the highest LTV.

- Report on your customers paying the most now.

- Sort your highest paying and lowest paying customers by date range.

- Segment your customers by specific products and categories of products they are interested in.

- Segment customers by their location and demographics.

Depending on your business, you can break this down even more. Consider all the extra sales you can make with this segmented approach. If you can sort your customer database by the top one hundred customers who buy during the holidays and make them a special bundle offer, this initiative will more than pay for itself. Once you have the data, you can run ads to them, send them emails, and also capture similar cold audiences.

KNOW YOUR CUSTOMER

An effective digital strategy starts with knowing who your customer is. Here are some questions to get you started:

- What are their pain points?

- What types of creative resonate with them?

- How do they respond to my specific creative output?

- How old are they?

- What sex are they?

- What is their income level?

- Where do they live?

- What are their interests?

- What is their time to purchase?

- What life events trigger their journey?

- What life events trigger a sale?

- What things do they hate and love?

- Who do they follow?

- What industry do they work in? Do they work at all?

- Where do they hang out?

- What events do they go to?

- What social media sites do they spend the most time on?

- What websites do they spend the most time on?

It is important to take the time to fill out all of this information about your customer. Based on this information, the slightest tweak to your creative, to your landing page, or to your audience could make or break your online business.

News Alerts

You can also waste a ton of budget if you don't pay attention to what's happening in the news. Is there a hurricane coming? Was there an earthquake? Were there wildfires?

This is an extreme example, but just to make a point:

when there are wildfires in Lake Tahoe, nobody in Northern California is buying houses—so, during the fire there's no point in spending $1 million a month on real estate ads in that region. An event like that would trigger paid media pauses in real estate ads, vacation ads, etc. However, the event could trigger an increase in ad spend in other industries, such as insurance in and around the region.

As part of any large-scale advertising operation, be sure to set up news delivery to everyone on the marketing team, allowing them to stay up on current events and pause an entire country, state, or city when appropriate. You can then reallocate that budget for an area where you'll get a better return. That flexibility represents the nuances of digital advertising; you can't shift gears so quickly with billboards or TV, but online, you can control the dial in an instant—but only if you're paying attention.

Get Local

One interesting aspect of running a large-scale national campaign is that your target varies widely by state. Customers in California are not the same as those in Texas, Florida, or New York. It never works as well to bring the same blanket message to each distinct region. Instead, it's better to customize the assets. Ignite Visibility won Search Marketing Campaign of the year for our customized work. Essentially, our team detected the location of each visitor in our ad network and served them an ad, and landing page, with their location as a keyword in the headline. The result? An over 280 percent increase in conversions for the client. All it took was something called "dynamic keyword insertion," which goes in the ads and landing pages.

To work effectively in the digital space, the best marketers use high-level visualization tools that will give them a sense not only of timeframe, but also regional breakdowns on the state-, city-, and even ZIP-code level. Google DataStudio is one of the best ways to visualize this data, but there are other options.

For certain campaigns, while ZIP code targeting might seem too narrow, the data says otherwise. After all, customer demographics can vary widely by neighborhood. Just look at the neighborhoods in your own city: affluent regions often sit adjacent to others that are not so well off—and therefore have much different customer profiles. Once you understand all the various mechanisms that contribute to your sales, you can set up an overall plan that drives more conversions. You might feel like you are going too small, but keep in mind it's all about the quality of the audience for your product or service. In San Diego where I live, for example, Mira Mesa is just a few miles away from La Jolla. Some of the wealthiest people in San Diego live in La Jolla. Mira Mesa, on the other hand, is very industrial and has more small businesses and modest homes. If you are trying to sell high-end art, which area would you target?

ASSEMBLE YOUR DIGITAL MARKETING TEAM

In the next section of the book, I'm going to touch on how to build your team. I've had the rare experience of exposure to thousands of marketing teams, ranging from a one-man show where the CEO does the marketing, to huge teams at multi-billion-dollar companies traded on the NYSE.

While working with all these companies, I've seen teams that are too small and some that are too big. But whether too big or too small, they almost all seem stressed. Part of this stress comes from the pressure they constantly receive to increase results, and part comes from the lack of program structure. To make sure your advertising team is set up properly, let's talk about your likely needs.

Here is a list of the different online channels you'll be launching at certain points:

- Organic social media

- PR and digital PR

- SEO

- Content

- Conversion rate optimization

- Data analytics

- Paid media

- Amazon and marketplaces

- Email marketing

- Website development and design

- Creative services

- Affiliate marketing

Now that you've seen this breakdown, here's a question for you:

What are the two things that connect all these channels—whether traditional (think TV and radio) or digital—together?

The answer: the offer (what you are offering in the ad) and the creative.

Keep these two elements in mind, because that's where any successful advertising team starts.

Looking back at the list, broadly speaking, all these functions can be grouped into one of six categories: earned media, paid media, owned media, analytics, conversion rate optimization, and affiliate marketing. It's important to have a strategy person, a project manager, and a support person for each one.

This may come as a surprise. Executives often think that it's enough to hire a single paid media person, for instance, when in reality they need a paid media person *for every different network they're on.* Sure, you can group a few networks together if you are a smaller company with a starter budget, but in general, someone who specializes in Google will not also excel at Facebook, and YouTube doesn't translate to LinkedIn. If you want to be the best in class on that network, then you need a subject-matter expert who understands that network deeply. To take this a step further, usually someone who specializes in e-commerce does not have the same skill set as someone in lead generation, media, information products, communities, local, apps, or another business line.

To assemble an effective digital marketing team, first designate an overall account strategist, someone who understands how to translate your goals and objectives into each marketing channel. Then, designate a specialist for each network. You have the option of hiring internally or hiring an agency. In most cases, companies will have internal marketing managers and hire agencies to run ads and do SEO, email, creative, and more to support the internal teams. Certain businesses may hire an agency for everything and others may pick and choose based on their strengths and preferences. We will get more into how to make that decision later.

From there, create a dashboarding system to track how each channel and contributor is performing. While in some ways comparing performance on Facebook to TikTok might seem like comparing apples and oranges, the workflows across platforms are often similar and the results certainly need to be weighed against each other for budgeting. Each network will need new creative, new landing pages, new audiences, and a systematic process to continually improve. Almost all operate off of persona, offer, audience, ad, impression share, impressions, CTR, clicks, conversion rate, conversions, revenue per conversion, and most importantly, CPA and ROAS.

Through dashboarding, you'll get a quick sense of whether your performance is unbalanced. If 50 or 60 percent of your business comes from Facebook or YouTube, then you have a huge liability. At any point in time, you could lose that channel and lose a high-risk percentage of your business. Even while the cost for a sale might be more expensive on another channel, it's worth it to diversify among five or more different sources of traffic to protect your business. If one channel goes away, you can always scale the others and have more sales. Also, the more major channels you are on, the better. If a customer sees you in multiple places, it only helps conversions. At a minimum, plan for quarterly meetings to review results and to adjust your plan moving forward. The only downside of too many channels is being spread too thin across them. This can cause you to run out of budget or result in too little data from any one platform algorithm. I have found that $800 a day is a good starter testing level for a new ad set and audience in a campaign.

Lastly, if you're looking at all this information and wondering how you can possibly scale your operation by hiring for an unmanageable amount of new roles, you're not alone. In fact, that's a major obstacle for most digital marketing operations. In almost no scenario does it make sense to have a full-time, in-house expert for each network, which is why companies rely on outside agencies with subject-matter experts. Remember: it's not just about having one expert. An expert also needs to have a boss who knows what they're doing to oversee the work and ensure there's a strategic program operating. Engaging an agency allows you to work with top talent (multiple experts), who work from defined methods, on multiple networks, in a cost-effective way.

The agency will have many experts in the same role, a training program, and the ability to work directly with the platform as a preferred partner—and, for any given platform, a good agency will understand that platform and have multiple clients working on it. For example, our agency is a premium partner with Yelp, TikTok, Amazon, Google, Facebook, Microsoft, and more. Each of these ad platforms gives us access to a team ranging from two to ten people and the ability to contact just about any division in their company. So, if we are going to launch a $5-million-a-month YouTube campaign or a $10,000-a-month Performance Max campaign, we have both our agency expertise and thorough platform support.

Overall, learn to work with your agency, appreciate your agency, and treat them like part of the team. Knowing how to manage an agency is critical for success. Don't manage by fear or threat. Make them love working on your account. You want them to feel like you are their favorite client. You and your agency should have a collaborative, energetic relationship where all ideas are welcome, and where winning is celebrated. Look out for your agency, and they'll look out for you.

BUILDING AN INTEGRATED SYSTEM

I've said it before, and I'll say it again: advertising on the internet is essentially like managing a financial portfolio.

Think about it. Everything online is an audience grab, which also makes everything online an asset. Everything is worth *something*. Let me break down this concept, because it's a very important one.

Apple isn't worth over $1 trillion today solely because it makes good phones and computers. They're one of the largest companies in the world because they also know how to build public sentiment through their many online assets: the Apple website, Apple News, Apple Music, even Apple communities on Facebook. Each of these assets fluctuates in value based on the amount of news, attention, and monetization, but they are all assets nonetheless.

To take that a step further, all the discussions about Apple fluctuate and have value as well:

- An iPhone fan Facebook group

- A fan-run Instagram account

- A blog post on the best iPhones of all time

- A top-ranking YouTube video about iPhones

- A Twitter feed that covers Apple news...you get the idea.

The value of these assets fluctuates as well: if news comes out that LeBron James was using Apple's latest iPhone at a Hollywood premiere, which would cause a surge in online attempts to buy the device, the value of all of these online assets about iPhones and Apple would also go up. That's because these online assets command attention that lead to the views, clicks, conversion rate, conversion, cost per conversion, ROAS, revenue, and customer LTV.

I first realized the connection between managing a digital ad campaign (or any online asset) and a financial portfolio when I was twenty-four. Fresh off my MBA, this perspective informed my work in the digital marketing world, allowing me to uniquely understand the big picture and connect pieces that other marketers often missed. I wasn't interested in simple Google rankings. Rather, I was interested in the larger micro- and macroeconomic forces and how those elements impacted the assets that already had online audiences. It's all connected! If you know how to look at the data, you can find everyone and everything that influences those audiences and calculate the value of each online asset.

This is the perspective I encourage you to adopt as you begin to think about marketing online. Where are your customers, really? And what do they need and want to see in an online asset? Understanding these questions is how you convert traffic for less money!

In other words, as you begin building out the framework of your digital marketing operation, remember the big picture. Digital advertising can now connect the entire customer lifecycle. Companies can map customer acquisition to business growth, staffing needs, availability of products, and product churn—and they can also create data visualization throughout the entire organization (see Chapter 5). I can't wait to speak about this more later in the book.

With an integrated perspective, marketing leaders can turn the knobs for digital marketing to meet specific business needs. Some of our clients are already doing this, using real-time communication to adjust their ad mix when production or supply chain issues require them to scale back in one area and scale up in another. That way, not only do they generate the most value for their marketing dollars, but they're also able to move the right products at the right time.

ACTION ITEMS

- Understand the current digital marketing land-scape and what that could mean for your marketing program.

- Be clear on your high-level business goals and priorities, as well as your specific marketing goals.

- Create a clear, actionable data management plan.

- Build out your customer profile. Identify their pain points, track the regional issues affecting your audiences, and determine the best way to connect with them.

- Assemble your digital marketing team, being careful to allocate dedicated owners for each marketing channel.

- Map all the assets in your space online, regardless if you can run paid media ads on them or not. You want to know where everyone is.

CHAPTER 5

VALUE-BASED BIDDING

Do you know who your most valuable customers are—and where they came from?

Not every customer brings the same value to your business. One might buy five products, while another might buy only one low-margin product. Another customer might want to buy your most expensive product, and still another customer might want to buy out all of your inventory and make you rich! All customers are not equal.

The good news? Marketers can now track all of these

scenarios, from the ad to the purchase. This practice is known as *value-based bidding*, and it's extremely exciting for many reasons.

Technically, the term "value-based bidding" is specific to Google, but the basic approach is possible for most platforms—including Facebook—with a little work. Here is the basic concept:

Once a buyer has made a purchase, marketers can track that purchase back to the specific ad that led to that purchase decision. From there, marketers in conjunction with the ad system operating with machine learning on autopilot rules, will take the ad, audience, and landing page used, and double down on those assets in the ad system. Through continued iterations, a brand's ads become more and more optimized, leading to increasingly better results. The coolest part is that the machine learning refinement of it is based on doubling down on the conversions that already led to the most value for your business.

As a premium Google Partner, I am proud to say our agency was not only one of the first to employ this strategy, but we're also a leader in client adoption.

Once the process has been built out, a well-structured value-based bidding program requires less manual work to maintain. After the system is in place, all you have to do is test new ads, audiences, landing pages, review recommendations, and then let your ad network's algorithm (machine learning) do the rest. Even if you don't do anything past this point, the machine will hypothetically improve results over time.

The challenge is setting up the program correctly. For value-based bidding to work, the investment comes upfront. Otherwise, you risk building a system that produces nothing more than vanity metrics—and as a result, you won't fully understand whether or why your ads are working.

Keep in mind that setting up value-based bidding and conversion tracking, in general, is critical for every business. You must take the time to do it. This book will not explain exactly how, because Google and each of the ad platforms provide their own resources on the process, and it's best to use their platform-specific documentation.

ASSIGNING VALUE TO LEADS

In less mature models, marketers track their success on basic metrics like CPC or CPA. While some data is better than no data, this information is shallow—and often misleading. Both CPC and CPA measure basic data, but not the target result. Did the user click through and then move on to something else, or did they make a high-value purchase? Or, if you get a lead, is it a qualified lead?

This question has led more mature marketing programs to move beyond CPC and CPA and start looking at metrics such as Cost of Sales (CoS) and, increasingly, return on advertising spend (ROAS). By focusing on ROAS, marketers are in essence bidding to a clear and meaningful value. In other words, when we think about bidding to value, we associate a specific, high-value outcome with clear business outcomes.

A ROAS-optimized campaign can be very useful for any business. However, to really drive value, the most mature digital marketing models take things one step further, maximizing not just the value of a conversion, but also the actual profit gained through that conversion.

Bidding to profit margin means prioritizing both the highest-margin products and highest-volume products (the ones you want to sell the most of), connecting the inventory in your supply chain with your ads, and then feeding that data back into the system to bid more efficiently.

Finally, the most mature strategy—which very few businesses are currently doing—is optimizing for customer LTV. I want to take a moment and emphasize this point: this is where all businesses want to get to, where they can connect customer LTV to their ad and refine their ads and inform the machine learning based on this number.

Whether you're seeking to drive more value by targeting ROAS, profit, or customer LTV, you can achieve these goals through a well-built value-based bidding program. The key is that you must actually have the necessary data to feed back into the ad system. Fortunately, most industry-leading CRM systems have begun building out their capacity to capture such data with the click of a button.

LEAD SCORING

A client we worked with used to judge its marketing team on whether it could secure at least 20,000 conversions every month. "Just get 20,000 leads a month, and we will be happy," said the hungry sales team.

The problem was that they were running two different offers, one of which captured poor quality leads, as only 50 percent of them didn't meet an essential qualification for becoming a client. Sure, the other half of these leads may convert, but if the marketing team took a step back and looked at the data, they

would see that 10,000 leads that poor really only mean 5,__ _
qualified leads. This brings up a key difference that I want to
make sure you remember. Write the following concepts down,
dog-ear your book, or bookmark your digital copy—whatever
it takes to keep these two concepts in your head:

- MQL: Marketing-qualified lead (MQL) is a potential customer that has been reviewed by the marketing team and satisfies the criteria necessary to
  be passed along to the sales team.[16]

- SQL: A sales-qualified lead (SQL) is a prospective
  customer who has moved through the sales pipe-
  line – from MQL through sales-accepted lead – to
  a position where the sales team can now work on
  converting them into an active customer.[17]

The previous scenario begged the question: Did our client
really need to target 20,000 conversions every month, or did
they just need a target for SQLs, which would allow them to
refine what they considered an MQL?

Let me answer the question for you:

- They needed to kill the offer that was delivering
  50 percent SQLs.

- They needed to create a new offer that delivered a
  larger percentage of SQLs.

Just by doing this, they cut the waste in their ad spend and
sales team's time by 25 percent. This allowed them to have a

---

16 "Marketing-Qualified Lead (MQL)," Gartner Glossary, accessed October 6, 2022,
https://www.gartner.com/en/sales/glossary/marketing-qualified-lead-mql-.

17 "Sales-Qualified Lead (SQL)," Gartner Glossary, accessed October 6, 2022, https://
www.gartner.com/en/sales/glossary/sales-qualified-lead-sql-.

smaller and less expensive sales team and close more business.

We took this a step further by testing five new offers, all new video, and image creative, and setting up ad sequencing, new landing pages, email nurturing, and more. But I'm getting ahead of myself. Let's step back to talk about lead quality.

Most marketers focus on the number of conversions or transactions rather than the quality of conversion, revenue per transaction, or customer LTV. I don't want to jump back and forth between e-commerce or lead generation too much here, so I am going to stick with lead generation. But keep in mind that these principles apply to both in the same way. Also, all e-commerce sites need a lead generation strategy in the form of...

Aggressive email captures.

Building first-party list data is critical for all businesses. So now, let's talk about lead scoring.

If you don't have a lead scoring system in place to make sure your team is driving *valuable* conversions to your business, then your marketing team is just chasing its tail—and losing money in the process.

Here's how lead scoring works. Let's say you have two different leads:

- **Lead 1.** Someone downloads a white paper on your website about development and design. You got a lead, but there's just one problem: you don't offer development and design services. **Lead score = 1.**

- **Lead 2.** Someone fills out a request to receive a consultation for paid media services and puts in a budget of $1 million a month. Not only are these precisely the services you offer, but the lead's budget is right in your target client range. **Lead score = 4. This is an SQL.**

Leads that fall somewhere in the middle are assigned a score of 2, 3, or 4 based on whatever metrics your team has prioritized.

I find it is best if you score your database using this method.

1. **Contact:** Information in the database without qualification

2. **Lead:** Someone who could be considered an MQL but has not been qualified

3. **MQL:** Someone who has entered through a marketing-qualified channel

4. **SQL:** A qualified customer who is interested in signing up and meets the sales criteria

5. **Deal:** A customer

Once you're collecting accurate data and scoring your leads properly, you can then refine your marketing toward the fives instead of ones. Then, through a value-based bidding approach, you will be able to target more customers through the algorithm.

FEED THE DATA BACK TO YOUR NETWORK

This third step is the key to value-based bidding's power. Many marketers have learned how to determine customer value, but they don't feed this information back into their ad network in order to optimize their campaigns. Through machine learning, the system is then able to determine which potential customers are most valuable and bid toward those customer profiles to deliver incremental revenue, uplift, and profitability to advertisers.

This is new territory for marketers. Google Ads has only recently begun collecting data on the value of one conversion over another. However, businesses that have used this approach have discovered endless opportunities for their campaigns—allowing them to maximize their marketing budget in a variety of ways, such as optimizing for products that drive the most profit, set different values across TV and PC accessories, set an average value of store visits before conversions (to let smart bidding maximize sales across all channels online and in-store), improve the quality of their leads, determine how much an online quote is worth versus contract signing, and more.

THE TIME TO ACT IS NOW

Value-based bidding works across all business models and gives marketers a better picture of their customers. No matter what model you're in—publishing, commerce, lead generation, local business—it works. Adding the value of conversion gives you much more robust reporting on metrics that matter to you and gives Google a clear view of how much your business values each customer.

Even better, this practice is so new that many of your competitors likely aren't doing it—meaning that if you embrace this approach, you immediately have an advantage.

To get started, look at your current tech stack and the systems you have in place. How is your tracking configured? What would it take to begin scoring leads? Then, how can you integrate value-based bidding and feed that information back into the ad system?

Continue to iterate and optimize this process, and eventually, you'll be optimizing not just for better margins, but for lifetime customer value—driving key business goals in the process.

As cookies continue to phase out, marketers simply won't have the same third-party data they had before. Through value-based bidding, you can use characteristics of your highest-valued customers to run ads to similar customers in the future.

Value-based bidding is a golden goose that everyone has been trying to achieve in marketing forever, and now, we can. If you want to keep up with the curve, then I strongly recommend moving your marketing efforts in this direction.

ACTION STEPS

- Set up effective offline tracking that ties a sale all the way back to the original marketing asset.

- Through lead scoring and other processes, determine the highest-value customers that not only drive the largest margins but also align with your business goals.

- Feed the data back into your ad platform to generate a better return through more focused targeting.

CHAPTER 6

TRACKING AND FORECASTING PERFORMANCE

Abusiness owner came to me saying he had a revolutionary way to challenge the auto market and $2 million a month to spend on digital marketing. That was exciting to hear at first—the prospect of a client needing to spend $24 million a year to grow a disruptive business would excite any agency.

As we started digging deeper, though, we realized

our new prospective client needed to do some work first. While he was certainly a smart person, he had not taken the time to forecast what the actual business model would look like.

Here's what we knew. The client wanted to launch a business to resell cars in an incredibly competitive market. That sounded reasonable enough, but there was a lot he didn't know—like the target CPA or cost per sale, how many cars he needed to sell in order to break even, or even what the competition looked like in the area. He also did not have the website set up or a good sales process. With so many unknowns, he was clearly jumping into something he had not thought through.

Now, could we make this all happen? Yes, we could have.

We could have built the website.

Added the inventory.

Determined what we needed to sell.

Determined the ad spend on each network needed to make that happen.

Calculated the rest of his business overhead.

Helped him with his operations setup.

Projected out sales and profit each month.

And so on.

But we didn't.

That is for the business owner to do before running ads. And when they have not done it first, at least on some level, it's a red flag.

Some of the biggest problems in digital marketing and business as a whole stem from having a bucket of money, unrealistic expectations, and no strategy. People jump into an initiative, only to look back a few months later and realize they haven't achieved the results they pictured.

They are excited. They know digital marketing works. So they say, "Take my money and make it happen!"

No way. Not me. I say show me the model first.

It's for these reasons that we've worked so hard to connect digital marketing to specific business models. Digital marketing sales will fuel your particular product or service but cannot make up for the lack of a solid business model, product, or service. Before allocating and spending a digital marketing budget, it's important to understand your comprehensive plan and how the pieces work together. Just as you would do for any good financial forecast, it's important to determine things like revenue per sale, profit margin, and ideal ROAS to break even, broken down by channel on a monthly, quarterly, and annual basis.

Most digital marketing agencies—and even internal marketing teams—won't run forecasts because they don't want to be liable. That disconnect represents a core problem in the industry. They will take your money, happy to have a client.

Without understanding how your business model ties to revenue and setting reasonable goals, all the marketing money in the world won't matter. If you're working with someone who won't tell you what your results will look like and instead only wants to sell you a flash in the pan, you know they don't have the necessary expertise or confidence in their product or service. In this chapter, you'll learn how to create a clear path to connect your business model to your marketing campaign.

THE BASICS

First, I am not going to teach you how to do overall business financial modeling and forecasting. I strongly recommend you work with a financial expert and/or read books such as *Traction* by Gino Wickman, *Good to Great* by Jim Collins, *Winning* by Jack Welch, and others so you can reconnect with the business basics.

Later in the chapter, we'll explore advanced approaches for managing your campaigns. But first, it's important that you're taking care of the marketing essentials. Keep all the following elements in mind as you begin to implement your marketing strategy, as they are an essential part of your checklist for running a successful, ongoing, digital marketing campaign.

Dashboards

The first thing you'll want is an easy-to-understand dashboard that will help you clearly see the returns you're getting for every single platform. These visualizations would include the following at a minimum:

- Conversions by network both for your small conversions and big conversions (micros and macros)

- Lead scoring

- New visitors

- Conversions broken down by MQL and SQL

- Revenue or leads

- Keyword rankings in Google

- Traffic and conversions by channel

- Traffic and conversions by source

- Traffic and conversions by campaign

- Types of conversions (i.e., phone calls, email captures, directions, leads, or revenue)

- Conversions by landing page

- Traffic by landing page

- Traffic source by landing page

- Traffic by website segment

There are tools available out there that can help you with dashboarding. Some of the most popular include:

- Google Data Studio

- Tableau

- NinjaCat

- Power BI

- Qlik

- TapClicks

- AdVerity

Each of those tools allows you to see all your KPIs (see below) and traffic levels in one place with a clear, visually appealing interface. I prefer Google Data Studio, coupled with a mechanism to populate that data, whether directly from the ad platform or with another application like Power BI or Adverity. If you go this route, make sure you are creating custom, in-depth, manual analysis on your campaigns at least monthly so you can spot trends.

Key Performance Indicators (KPIs)

What are the key performance indicators (KPIs) you'll be using to measure your campaign's success? If you don't have KPIs for every single campaign, then how will you know whether you've succeeded or not?

Here's how to establish KPIs for your campaign:

- **Brainstorm.** Common KPIs include views, view duration, impression share, CTR, conversion rate, conversions, lead, MQL, SQL, deal, cost per conversion, cost per impression (CPM), ROAS, average order value, transactions, lifetime customer value, total revenue, and new visitors. However, be wary of simply copy-and-pasting competitor or others' KPIs and using them as your own. The goals for your campaign may be very different from the goals of another company.

- **Establish regular reviews.** The KPIs you start with may not be the ones you end up with. Scrutinize every single KPI constantly to ensure it's giving you valuable information. Remember, seasonality plays a significant role in your results. Compare your results to those from the previous month, quarter, and year. Quarterly business reviews are especially critical. How did everything go over the last quarter? What were the big initiatives, and what will the big initiatives be moving forward? How will you beat what you did last quarter and in the same quarter last year?

- **Run forecasts on a monthly basis.** The last week of the month, you should forecast your conversions by channel for the next month and consider how they align with your overall conversion goals. You can use predictive modeling through a tool like Google Data Studio, Adverity, or our software at Ignite Visibility, which is called CertaintyTech, or you can create a manual media plan based on your current KPIs. Regardless of the approach you choose, you will want to watch your key metrics and forecast every month, quarter, and year. We'll discuss forecasts later in the chapter and why they are so valuable to performance.

When it comes to KPIs, too many people focus on overall sessions, which is not a useful metric. Actual conversions are most important, broken down by top landing page and website segment. Sometimes returning members inflate traffic growth, so make sure you can parse the membership and nonmembership sections of your website to identify actual new visitors. I also recommend using the Google Analytics Intelligence Events function, which will alert you to anomalous drops or increases in traffic. Some alerts are AI-driven, and you can also set your own custom ones, such as when there's a 20 percent drop in traffic for a landing page.

Creative

In the next chapter, we'll take a deep dive into producing effective creative for your campaigns. Equally important to producing good creative is tracking it.

Phase out the poor creative and make more of the good creative.

Marketers often make the mistake of analyzing creative based on platform alone. "How did this creative perform on YouTube versus Facebook?" they ask. This question can be useful, but to get the full story, it's essential to break down your performance on an overall creative level. Specifically, you will want to compare the performance of different pieces of creative and make future decisions accordingly.

For example, imagine you have two pieces of advertising creative for a surfboard. One is a video of a guy surfing with text that says, "Buy now." The other is an image of a guy surfing with text that says, "The best surfboard on the planet." To compare these two pieces of creative, regardless of which platform they run on, you want an idea of their overall KPIs, as measured by impressions, CTR, conversion rate, and ROAS. For any piece of creative, you need those KPIs across platforms as well against each other on the same platform.

Comparing that data, you'll start to see trends in which asset has a much better click-through, conversion rate, and ROAS than the other. When you identify the stronger performer, pause the weaker one and swap in something new, to test iterations of the stronger performer, such as with different language and images. Using that strategy, you can convert traffic for less. I'll get more into this later.

Forecasts

When you're forecasting, there are a few things you need to keep in mind. First, what did your channels do last year? Next, are you trending above or below that currently? You also need to consider past anomalies and increases or decreases in each channel.

There are essentially three ways to look at projections.

- **Linear.** If there wasn't any seasonality or an applied growth rate, what would your digital marketing look like for the rest of the year, as a flatline basis for the amount of business you'd bring in? I like to look at the linear baseline. Tell yourself, "Okay, if we kept doing exactly what we are doing, this is what it would look like."

- **Growth Rate.** This type of analysis shows you how much you'd continue to grow in each channel based on your current pace. If you've converted 10 percent better every month, organic traffic has been growing by 10 percent each month or you've been increasing ad spend by 10 percent every month, you can decide whether you want to continue modeling out growth for that channel based on the same trend.

- **Seasonality.** For many brands, the holidays are completely different from Q1 or Q2. A good forecasting model accounts for this. If you are modeling out for Q4, and last year you had an organic surge in customer sales of 30 percent in Q4, you want to take that into account and capitalize on it.

Smart marketing operations look at annual marketing spend and revenue forecasts the same way finance looks at overall company annual forecasts. For these organizations, these forecasts are granular, looking at seasonality and growth-rate projections based on the last two or three years and accounting for any anomalies or black swan events. In the next section, we'll show you just how deep down the forecasting hole your organization can go.

THE FORECASTER METHOD

Once you have your basic tracking in place, you can scale and spend money much more confidently. I've written an entire book on this subject called *The Forecaster Method,* which gives you the framework for the perfect digital marketing system. If you're interested in exploring this topic in greater depth, I recommend picking up that book as well. The book is for sale on Amazon.

In this section, I'll walk you through the basics of one section of the book, which is the Forecaster Method model.

The basic idea of the Forecaster Method is to take all your different marketing channels and pit them against each other. You want to look at the total cost, traffic, conversion rate, conversion LTV, CPA, revenue generated, ROAS, and then the percent of your portfolio. Based on those metrics, you can decide whether or not to scale a specific channel.

To do that, create an ongoing, systematic approach to scaling different channels until they all have an equal contribution margin based on ROAS. For example, if you notice Facebook and Instagram have a low ROAS, you might not want to scale that channel. If display and discovery have a good

ROAS and represent less than 10 percent of the portfolio, you might want to scale that area. Leveling out ROAS over time offers a way to develop the best system for long-term digital marketing growth with the highest return and lowest cost.

For the Forecaster Method to work, you'll need to have a marketing presence on at least five different traffic sources, each at less than 30 percent of your total budget, based on the saturation point for each channel. Then, you will review each of these channels monthly based on the key metrics, and then scale accordingly.

If you're not sure how to allocate your budget per channel, here are some suggestions:

- Learn from your competitors. How much are they spending and where are they spending it? You can use tools such as ispot.tv, Similar Web, SpyFu, Pathmatics, or SEMRush to determine this. Also, if you're a Google Premier Partner like us, Google will provide you with all the data you need here.

- Determine how much revenue you need to drive the business

- Create a model of your CPA and ROAS for each channel.

- Determine how much you need to spend, how big the audience size is, what your CTR would be, what your conversion rate would be, what your cost per conversion would be, and what your ROAS would be.

There is some complexity to the process. There is an optimal level for each platform before it becomes less profitable—which means each channel can only be scaled so much before your attempts to maximize output produce diminishing returns. For instance, it wouldn't make any sense to allocate 30 percent of your budget to Google search if there are only a few thousand searches a month in a category. That would be an awareness play, and you would need another network.

With the Forecaster Method, your goal is to understand the optimal amount to spend on each channel, fully maximize it, and then move on. In some cases, you end up with six or seven different channels you're spending on. The goal is to constantly expand until you've maxed out a channel and there's no more inventory that can drive conversions within your KPI goals.

For example, if you're using Facebook, you might find that you drive the optimal ROAS when you spend $160,000. If you go to $180,000, your ROAS could drop from 400 percent to 200 percent. Although your sales and revenue go up, your cost per sale also goes up. Your ad spend has increased, but the number of conversions doesn't scale at the same rate.

Understand the law of diminishing returns for each channel, and then weigh it against the overall portfolio. You can determine the right mix easily as long as you have accurate metrics. As we discussed in the previous chapter on value-based bidding, once you have dialed this process in, the next step is to progress beyond ROAS and get into gross profit, profit margin, and then lifetime customer value.

Just to give you an example portfolio, a lead generation company might look something like this.

- Google Search: $150,000 a month, 300 percent ROAS

- Google Display: $10,000 a month, 300 percent ROAS

- Google Discovery: $10,000 a month, 300 percent ROAS

- YouTube: $50,000 a month, 300 percent ROAS

- Facebook: $30,000 a month, 300 percent ROAS

- LinkedIn: $20,000 a month, 300 percent ROAS

- Programmatic: $50,000 a month, 300 percent ROAS

Lead the Pack

In my experience, only about 1 percent of companies in the world have set up everything I've outlined here; I'm including those with and without a digital program. When they do have a digital program, only 40 percent of companies have their tracking set up right (and even fewer have it set up to the extent that I outlined in this chapter). Only 30 or 40 percent have high-quality data visualization and dashboards. Fewer than 10 percent of companies have any type of systematic monthly forecasting, and only 1 or 2 percent have any type of value-based bidding.

I've outlined the best, most innovative practices that even many of the best brands in the world haven't reached at this point yet. Some don't even realize the capabilities that exist or how much they're leaving on the table by not having an expert get them squared away. Usually, the ones that have this setup right are sophisticated e-commerce or lead generation businesses that primarily do business online. Also, they're usually spending more than $20,000 a month on online ads. When the ad spend goes up, more people in the organization start looking at it, and tracking, visualization, forecasting, networks, conversion rate optimization, and creative become highly visible.

Plenty of companies are still flying blind. They're running ads for clicks, with no knowledge of true customer conversions. They don't have a good handle on their data. They don't know if what they're counting as a "lead" is truly an SQL. They look at some data through their ad platform, and others through their CRM. The pieces aren't connected. Their ad platform says they got 2,000 leads and their CRM says three, but only one is an SQL, and everyone is confused. No more! Follow the methods in this book! Report on true customer sales not vanity metrics like video views. That is the challenge to all of you over the next year.

People think digital is a much better advertising option than TV, radio, or billboards because you get all this data on clicks, but none of that matters. What really matters is the final sale, which is where the next evolution of the web will focus. And in that regard, if you implement what I've outlined here, then you'll be light years ahead of the pack. (P.S., Digital is not necessarily better than TV, radio, or billboards. It's just a different animal.)

ACTION ITEMS

- Set up data visualization and KPIs within and across campaigns, and conduct regular reviews and deep dives.

- Make sure you're tracking the effectiveness of your creative—not just across channels, but with the actual content itself.

- Create robust forecasts for how you expect your marketing efforts to play out over the next month, quarter, and year.

- Using the Forecaster Method, determine how much of your budget you should allocate to each channel before any initial investment leads to diminishing returns.

CHAPTER 7

CREATIVE AND AUDIENCES

A major brand that had been spending $8 million per year on online advertising approached us because they were frustrated with their last agency, which had not delivered on their promises. When we audited the account, we quickly realized why. The ads running were testimonials shot a couple of years earlier, hadn't been refreshed, and were not up to any version of modern paid social standards: poor-quality video, poor lighting, and very basic text that essentially just said, "Buy now." Clearly, they needed a creative refresh.

To start, we wanted to understand their business more

and how their customers connected with them. Explaining this was no sweat for their team, who shared an inspirational story about the owner that reflected positively on the entire organization and its core values. We then matched this data from a study on the industry. The study discussed the three biggest customer concerns:

1. The product should greatly protect the environment. Prospective customers weren't very concerned with price; they cared more about the planet and the impact of the product.

2. Time spent using the product. Many customers felt it would take too long to use and were not aware of recent advancements.

3. Novel industry. Customers were concerned the industry would go away, and the need for the product would evaporate.

Armed with such a rich story from the owner, and clear customer concerns, we got to work. First, we created a storyboard for top-level creative that described the overall company mission. Then, we created a series of new direct conversion-based ads with bright colors and good calls to action. Next, we redid all the testimonial ads to better align the company with both their story and their customers' most pressing pain points. Finally, we created a new set of urgency ads to help capture more attention.

With this new collateral, we restructured the brand's entire organizational approach on their site so that prospects saw these elements in a sequence, from the introductory story to products or services, to testimonials, to final conversion-based ads. The new creative achieved a 40 percent lift in sales, without the company having to increase ad spend. It was simply an investment of $20,000 to refresh their creative.

One of the biggest mistakes we've seen in digital marketing over the years is good ad targeting done with bad or outdated creative. New ad systems run on algorithms that pick the best creative and show it more, in an iterative cycle. If you don't feed in high-quality, fresh material, then you will not receive the impression share that you should, which will result in a low CTR. As a result, creative has become more important in paid media than ever before. In this chapter, you'll learn how to create smart, effective creative that will continue to add value all along the buyer's journey.

APPROACHING THE MARKETING FUNNEL

Broadly speaking, the top of the funnel is for broader marketing appeals for customers just starting out on their journey. As your prospective customers move down the funnel, some will continue to show interest, while others will drop out. To keep customers moving forward, your messaging should become increasingly targeted and focused on driving a buying decision.

Naturally, to meet your buyers at different stages of the funnel, you'll need to craft different types of creative. Often, however, you can still use the same channels.

For instance, search can be valuable at any point in the

funnel, but the messaging will change depending on the stage. Take a company selling mountain bikes online. Search terms for customers at the top of their funnel would be simple, such as "how to mountain bike." Once a customer has moved down the funnel, something like "best mountain bikes" would be better. At the bottom of the funnel, "buy a mountain bike on sale" may be more appropriate. That approach to keywords within search translates to video search engines, such as YouTube, as well.

This is where good creative becomes so important in managing your marketing funnel. Because cookies will soon be a thing of the past (see Chapter 3), the new goal is to retarget prospective customers via compelling, content-based offers. For instance, buyers at the top or mid-funnel might benefit from an expert's mountain-biking guide to the best trails in the world. You could offer such a guide in exchange for the buyer's email address, which then gets that person in your database.

Generally, at the top of the funnel, your goal is simply to generate awareness for your brand and what you want to be known for. You can cast a wide net here; if a thousand people were in the room, could you get a hundred of them to view your ad? This is the goal of creative on channels like display and YouTube—raising awareness, engaging more people, and creating a positive initial association for your brand.

As we've discussed throughout the book, the goal is to become proficient at one channel, maximize your potential, and then move on. Continue systematically through the process until all the channels are working. Your overall portfolio is like a pie chart, and each slice makes a different contribution to your specific, bottom-line goals.

CUSTOMER JOURNEY MAPPING

The marketing funnel represents how someone first becomes aware of a brand and eventually becomes a customer—and, in some cases, how they're no longer a customer. Customer journey mapping is a bit different. Through this process, marketers can lay out all the various ways a buyer would ever interact with their brand and then work to ensure that those buyers convert for the least expense and the highest return.

First, mapping looks at the top traffic sources:

- Are those traffic levels and conversion rates where they should be?

- What are your top pages and funnels?

- Is there a high bounce rate?

Then, mapping looks at all your marketing channels and every way you impact the customer through those marketing channels and then documents the journey.

For instance, say you're managing your email channel. To map your customer's journey, ask:

- How do they first enter your email list?

- How do they get their first, second, third, and fourth automation?

- Which landing page did they come from or hit?

- What happened when they converted?

- What is their post-conversion automation?

This is just one example. Sophisticated organizations map the entire customer journey for each channel: email, paid media, SEO, social media, affiliate marketing, and every other channel out there. In some cases, they also try to create an omnichannel customer journey map, affording them the capacity to be more deliberate with their funnel and optimize results. In the following sections, I'll teach you the basics of how to set up your own customer journey mapping process.

How to Map

When navigating the customer journey mapping process, here are the steps I recommend:

1. Look at all of a client's different channels—social, organic, paid search, direct email, display, referral events, podcasts, affiliates, and so on.

2. Examine the users, new users, bounce rate, conversion rate, and goal completions.

3. Determine whether the traffic and conversion rate are high enough. If yes, great; if not, how can you increase those? If you have a high traffic source but a low conversion rate, how can you improve that conversion? If it's a low traffic source but a high conversion rate, you should allocate more money to grow that channel.

My team and I go through that process systematically, not just for the client's channels, but also for different media (like organic traffic) and sources (like Google). Then, we address ways to improve the poor and moderate performers while spending even more with the best performers. Landing page performance also factors in.

Once you have all the information, you can employ certain tactics—such as moving the call to action (CTA) up on the page, optimizing for mobile, testing headlines, or refining the audience for better traffic quality—in order to improve the conversion rate. If you would like to learn more about conversion rate optimization, we have a free one-hour course on our YouTube channel called "Learn Conversion Rate Optimization."

Choosing the Right Tool

To execute on this process and make sure we're working with the best, most robust data, we use Google Analytics 4 as our primary tool, which has a few distinct advantages over other similar tools.

The primary advantage is that Google Analytics 4 provides user behavior flow reports, which essentially does some of the customer journey mapping work for you. You can select any or all sources of traffic and connect them to any page on the website, and the tool will generate a visual representation of click-throughs, final conversions, and drop-off rates.

This is invaluable information. If there's a high drop-off rate, for example, you might want to revise your call to action, refine your messaging or value proposition, or fire an exit pop-up on those pages. Or, you might want to include a survey on that page soliciting user opinions regarding whether they're getting all the information they need. If you're still not sure what the problem is, you could even use a website like Try My UI, which has real people test your pages and allows you to watch them.

Google Analytics also helps you determine how long it takes from initial contact until conversion. On some sites, people might convert the first time, and on others, it might take multiple website visits and months of time. However, running ads for a longer remarketing window of 60 to 120 days could result in even more conversions on the back end. In the B2B and retail spaces, we're seeing longer and longer time lags until conversion. Understanding your average cycle can inform your ad and remarketing strategies to maximize effectiveness. But generally, companies don't have long enough retargeting windows set up.

Finally, the last big advantage of Google Analytics is that it allows you to set your conversion path. You can see if most of your users convert the first time on one traffic source and what the path looks like for people who have two, three, or four touchpoints that brought them to the website. Maybe your biggest conversion path is someone who comes in through organic search but then returns from a paid ad. If so, you might add a coupon or discount to that paid ad to increase the number of conversions from that path. You also want to ensure that organic gets credit for generating the lead or sale, opposed to attributing it all to paid simply because it got the last click.

Other benefits of Google Analytics include:

- Sort by source, so you can see which traffic comes from Google, Instagram, Facebook, and elsewhere, where people go, and which aspects aren't working.

- Track customer touchpoints.

- Create different reports, such as the multichannel

conversion report and assisted conversions report function.

The assisted conversion report is especially valuable, showing you how many traffic sources assisted in a conversion, meaning they weren't the last click but played a role at some point during the conversion process. If the last click wasn't from Google but Google assisted with 5,000 conversions, then it's still an important, primary piece of traffic you should spend time on.

Using the Map

Once you have all this information in place, what does the tactical perspective look like? How do you really place ads in all the right touchpoints?

Let me give you an example:

Imagine again you're trying to sell mountain bikes. Based on the data, you determine that your best approach is to identify the top influencers in the world on mountain biking, the top YouTube channels, and the top news sites, and advertise on those channels. Then, you might seek out not just the top channels, but the top *videos* on mountain biking—the ones that have five million, ten million views, or more.

Now, when you are looking at the content on these online assets, you want to ask yourself the following:

- Who are the top influencers?

- What is the top type of concept people are consuming?

- What are the top articles in the news publications?

- What content is not only getting the most traffic but also the most engagement? (Consider this your bottom-line question.)

Once you have those answers, you could consider advertising directly on those specific pieces of content, offering great ways to spend money inside an ecosystem with a high probability of conversion. You may also decide to create similar content yourself to use in your online ad messaging and content marketing.

Please take a moment to consider what I just said. If you actually do this strategy, you will have success. It is one of the most effective advertising tactics possible. People just run blanket ads across poor network targeting and their businesses go under as a result. This targeted approach makes the difference.

As you can see in this example, customer journey mapping starts with the customer, determines quality networks, and then finds the specific places within those networks that are the highest assets. Once you've mapped out all those relevant options, you can think about where you want to spend the most money and which networks should have the highest budget. Where should you be bidding the most? For example, those top ten YouTube videos might cost five to twenty dollars per thousand impressions for highly niche pieces of content—higher bids than other more general options. With the right data, you can determine whether that expense is worth it or whether it's better to hold your marketing dollars for somewhere else.

The customer journey does not stop there. It also involves the website. At the end of the day, you want to map the entire process:

Customer > Network > Audience > Content Placement > Ad > Landing Page or Native Form

DEVELOPING YOUR CREATIVE

Creative messaging is critical to your overall marketing strategy. You must define the main concepts you want to portray and the pillars of your creative strategy. Also, you'll need to determine how your strategy fits into the different content buckets and then look at those buckets and how they should be utilized at the top of the funnel all the way to the bottom of the funnel.

Once you have the buckets, you should create your concept, and then source the content. There are a lot of questions to consider:

- What's your content, and what's your script?

- What is the mood of your content, and what is your basic approach?

- Will you use custom art or archived stock footage?

- What about high-end impact music that aligns with the brand and creates brand consistency?

The best creative content is intentional. Be deliberate and invest the time to do creative well. Today's landscape requires more sophistication than simply writing out a bit of copy and spinning out content from that. The best marketers put the time into developing great creative and compelling offers, something that will connect with their audiences.

In other words, plan your approach, and then *create good ads*. Five or ten years ago, you could slap something together and get decent reach, but now the platforms algorithmically drive what does well. There's a combination of art, science, and psychology to find the right mix to target your customer within a given platform. In the following sections, we'll explore the many considerations for producing strong, consistent content:

Positioning Your Brand

Before you create any specific assets, make sure you are clear on the following:

- Buyer personas
- Buyer pain points
- Your product's unique value proposition
- Unique selling angles
- Key differentiators

To begin gathering this data, look at the qualities of the people who have converted inside of Google Analytics. You can find out where they're from, their top interests, their age, their gender, how many times they've come to the website, type of mobile or desktop device they're using, the city or country they're in, and where they came from on the web—whether from a social media site, search engine, or news publication.

I recommend using all the analytics platforms in addition

to Google—Facebook, YouTube, Twitter, etc.—and then investing time in building personas based on the conversion data to create a detailed picture of the exact demographics of the person you target online. Then, when you set up your paid media targeting, you can select those exact qualities in your audiences. For example:

- If you build an audience inside of Google and want to run ads to your website, you can use your highest-converting audience qualities for your Google ads, leading to much higher-quality traffic.

- On Facebook, if you know who your audience is and who they're the biggest fans of, you can run ads on the audiences of fan pages. Facebook also allows you to create unique audiences based on fans of other pages or groups. All you have to do is invest the time to learn what else your customers are subscribed to.

Before you do that, of course, you need to create a set of three to five clear buyer personas. Build these personas correctly, and you should be able to account for 90 percent of the purchases for your business.

First, get a broad sense of who your persona is. If you're a marketing company, for instance, one persona might be "Jenna," a forty-two-year-old CMO of a company in California who enjoys reading *Ad Age* and *TechCrunch*, boating, and watching action movies.

From there, you'll want to determine your persona's pain points. The best way to determine these is to ask your customers directly, such as with Google Forms, SurveyMonkey, or a survey tool on your website like Hotjar. Other tools like AnswerThePublic, Semrush, and the Google "People Also Ask" box will reveal the main questions your customers are asking, along with the search volume. Knowing your buyer's personas and their pain points gives you huge leverage to target your messaging.

Finally, using this information, you can begin to build out your value proposition, unique selling angles, and key differentiators. If you're not sure what makes you stand out, read through some competitor reviews—both the positives and the negatives—to look for trends. Based on the frequently cited negatives (e.g., lack of customer service, cost, or lack of specific features), you can market yourself as addressing those issues.

Once you've considered all these data points and how you fit into the market, write up a clear description of your persona. This description should be about 100 to 150 words, listing out their basic demographic information, their likes and interests, their pain points, and what they're looking for in your product or service.

From there, it's time to put this knowledge into action. Here are a few examples how:

- Input keywords around your product or service into tools like Google Trends. This will allow you to determine whether search traffic around a product or service is going up or down and whether there are new breakout segments of that product or service, which you can also view by region. This will allow you to see rising trends your persona might be searching for.

- Design your website to pass the seven-second test. When someone visits your page, they should know within seven seconds who you are, what you do, and what your key differentiators are—and they should see a call to action. All these elements combined drive conversions on your website and speak to your persona.

The more time you invest in addressing these considerations, the more value you'll reap. Too often, people don't strategize upfront; instead they haphazardly jump to making ads, picking audiences, and launching campaigns. As a result, they waste tens of thousands of dollars or even fail as a business. Take the time to lay the groundwork first, and you'll have bigger, faster results down the road. Also, make sure you revisit each element quarterly to keep iterating.

Writing Good Copy

Content is king and bad copy leads to zero sales. Companies that cheap out on copywriting and don't put in the time to perfect the messaging always pay for those shortcuts later. Unfortunately, this problem is rampant. Brands regularly underestimate the value of writing good copy and, in many cases, don't update the copy on their website for years.

For example, one client came to us trying to figure out why their website wasn't converting. They couldn't understand it—they had a beautiful site, offered good service, were making fine money, and had a decent set of clients and thousands of website visitors a month. But as beautiful as their site was, the homepage didn't describe what they offered. People who came to their site had no idea what their business did.

You've probably seen companies that do this—there are many prominent examples to choose from. WeWork, for instance, said for a long time their mission was to "elevate the world's consciousness." But they actually provide shared office space solutions and you would never know that from their mission statement. Why not something like, "Shared office space at an affordable price"? To their credit, as of this writing, their home page says, "Get 50 percent off WeWork All Access. Work from anywhere with access to hot desks worldwide with one monthly membership." So, at some point, their marketing team got a little more conversion-focused.

When it comes to writing good copy, a couple of words in an ad or on a landing page can make the difference between making or missing out on millions of dollars. It's essential to accurately describe what you do, the key benefits, your offers, and what you want the user to do—all tying back to brand positioning.

Once again, testing on a regular basis is essential to getting this right. Recently, we saw a 35 percent lift in conversions for one of our larger clients simply by changing one sentence on their landing page. Considering that this client runs millions of dollars a year to this landing page, 35 percent represented a huge bump for them.

Effective copy starts with a callout that captures your audience's attention right off the bat, encouraging them to think, "Yes, this is what I'm looking for." What's a big problem in your customer's life that your product or service can solve? Tell a story, capture their attention, pose a big problem, and then build up to and provide a solution. In the buildup, explain how it took so long to find this solution, describe all the trials and tribulations, list why it's valuable and the best option, and name everyone who contributed to it.

Good copy also borrows devices from blockbuster movies—it presents your product or service as the hero, having cut through the problems and pain to offer a solution. Once you've championed it as the hero, break down the barriers that might make people resistant. Emphasize ease of use, speed, value for the investment, credentials and benefits compared to competitors, and social proof (i.e., a track record of successful users).

Once you have the customer on board with all those benefits, a good copywriter pushes them over the top by offering additional bonuses they may not have expected. Make it an offer no one would even consider saying no to. Then, you can inject scarcity, such as a limited run or a temporary price drop, followed by a call to action. Close your copy by warning what will happen if the person doesn't buy now, reiterating the key reasons why your product or service is the hero, and making an extra offer.

If all of this sounds like the elements of a sales letter, you're right. It's a proven formula that works, and yet 99 percent of websites don't follow this formula. Instead, they use vague language and fail to guide the visitor toward the desired action, and they leave money on the table as a result. I want to give credit to Perry Belcher here, who is a peer of mine and an excellent digital marketer. Much of this formula came from his tips.

Storyboarding

Successful campaigns use high-impact, heavily edited, story-boarded ads with creative direction, varied by position in the funnel. They consistently nurture people over time until they reach the final conversion process. As they say, good creative is the last unfair advantage in digital marketing.

Through a series of slides, the storyboard illustrates how you'll nurture the customer from the beginning of the creative until the end and how you'll convert. For each concept, set up a storyboard of anywhere from three to ten slides, laying out each of the different pillars. Think about the sequence of how you're making the creative. For instance:

- **Initial slides (1–3):** Something that is both eye-catching and that explains the buyer's pain point.

- **Middle slides (3–6):** You'll expand on the problem and end with all the product's benefits.

- **Final slides (7–10):** Your call to action (CTA). What do you want your buyer to do?

The storyboarding process will give the video editor or designer a direction for making the creative. It allows you to create any type of video or animation and make multiple versions. You can chop up the footage and test a flight to find the best response. If you run six versions, the ad platform will naturally gravitate toward the one with the best impression share, CTR, engagement rate, and video view duration.

While text and image ads used to be enough, now video is the main medium. In 2022 alone, online video was expected to make up 82 percent of consumer internet traffic. Videos, in general, achieve a CTR much higher than text. Broadly speaking, this makes video the strongest option for advertising, but only if you can crack the code, create good video, and offer content people want to interact with. The creative direction comes down to thinking about who the customer is, which pillar you're pursuing, and where they are in the journey—then you produce a script and storyboard, film a raw video, and edit it.

Story-based ads are usually fifteen seconds or less, while an ad on YouTube can be longer. We've seen success with both long-form ads of thirty seconds to ten minutes on YouTube, as well as very short-form ads on YouTube, TikTok, and Reels, in some cases as short as five or ten seconds.

Whatever the case, it's important that your team understand what works and where so that you can maximize the effectiveness of your campaign.

The goal is to crack that code and get viewers to digest all the content. Long or short, it doesn't matter. What matters is that it converts. The only thing to note here is that if it's short, a viewer might be more likely to watch the entire thing. This is why short videos are best for direct, lower-funnel offers and for getting your brand known. For example, if you are running a five-to-ten-second ad, you can simply say your brand name and include a call to action.

Brand Equity

As you're developing your creative, you'll also want to consider your brand equity. Ask:

- What's your brand already known for, and how can you leverage that?

- What are your competitors doing, and what seems to be working and not working for them?

- What type of content is your audience already consuming online, and what's trending in their space?

- Are there specific themes going on within your consumer base, inside or even outside your industry, that you can align with? (For example, Chipotle has aligned with avocado marketing, and the avocado industry has also done a great job with its own marketing. The two have joined forces and done cross-channel video marketing on their different social media sites, to good effect.)

Evergreen Concepts

What could you include in your design, concept, and sourcing that will always work? Examples include:

- Free consultations
- Testimonials
- "About" videos
- Product-demo videos
- Explainer videos
- White papers
- Download videos
- Discount codes

- Special offers and promotions

- Problem-and-solution videos

- Powerful storytelling videos

In some cases, you can create an effective evergreen ad that drives your whole strategy. Some ads get such wide reach that you only need one really good piece of creative to build an entire business. We actually have an ad like this at Ignite Visibility. Just turn it on, and it drives business.

A friend of mine built a $50 million dollar business from one ad and one landing page. He focused on a clear funnel with excellent creative and a quality system, rather than spraying a bunch of mediocre content online without targeting. If you invest the time to make something good, you'll find that you'll need to invest much less time down the road.

Leveraging Events

Events are another effective marketing strategy. While they take a little more work, they can result in a spike in sales and a new customer base. Over the course of the year, map out specific events in your industry, beyond the regular holidays. Have a plan in place for unique creative events around those events that you can release in the thirty to ninety days leading up to them. Scale your ads accordingly and use tools like countdown timers to increase the urgency around unique opportunities.

At a minimum, we recommend hosting an event once per quarter. In some cases, and even for our own business, we like to do an event once a month. Make sure you set up a good CPA framework to attract people to these events in order to increase attention toward your business, develop more thought leadership, and grow your potential customer list.

Events are a way to re-engage customers, advertise to people who have not yet converted, and reach new audiences. It's a good idea to invite people who have purchased a product or service before, as well as those who have filled out a form but have not yet made a purchase. When you do event marketing, you also capture new first-party data that you can use to nurture people until they eventually become customers.

Scale the size of the events over time, starting with twenty or thirty people, increasing to a couple hundred, and eventually reaching the thousands. The goal is to keep growing the event size and plan a better calendar each year. The best event topics come from the biggest pain points in the industry—seasonally, based on current events, related to prevailing economic conditions, and so on. Bring in outside experts who are not competitors but are also seen as thought leaders in the industry, which allows you to cross-market to their customer list as well.

Working with Influencers

Influencers have reached the same level of perception as celebrities, so influencer-based creative often works quite well. Work with influencers and create partnerships whenever creative is slow. Who are the top influencers in your industry that aren't competitors? Bring them into your advertisements, do interviews with them, and show them with your product or service in demo videos.

Having a group of from five to fifty influencers who promote your product or service when you have a new launch—or on a consistent basis—allows you to get in front of their audience and gain more customers and conversions. You should use your influencers on a monthly basis; results will scale with consistency.

One of the best strategies is to use ad networks to advertise to influencers' audiences. If your customers like a particular influencer, you can get the influencer's permission to advertise to everyone who follows their account. Include the influencer's name and image in your ad to signal alignment with your brand.

We've used this strategy with quite a few influencers for great success. It's mutually beneficial to you and the influencer to have access to each other's audiences. I cannot tell you how much better the results are using this strategy opposed to using a network-provided, audience-targeting strategy.

DIFFERENT TYPES OF CREATIVE

When it comes to producing different types of creative content, consider the different stages of the customer's journey. Some people are new to the brand. Others know about the brand but haven't visited the site yet. Some people have visited your site but haven't converted. There are those who have visited the site and actually converted, but they haven't become customers. Finally, there are previous customers to whom you can sell a different product or service. Once you break prospects down into these different segments, you can set up a landing page and an ad strategy specific to those positions in the funnel.

To give an example of how this might play out, imagine someone is completely new to your brand. Your first goal is to introduce yourself and allow that person to learn a little bit more about you. Then you'd pursue a micro-conversion strategy, such as offering a download for a white paper, a webinar with an introductory discount, or a free giveaway. Those offers allow you to collect data and get the person into the email nurturing system. If you have the functionality enabled, you can also cookie them (for the time being). If they hit the site and haven't converted, they'll receive ads and emails to push them further down the funnel.

Think about matching your creative from top to bottom and then by audience segment. Your creative requires variations tailored to each step and segment, from introduction all the way to conversion, post-conversion, and then cross-selling.

The Value of Storytelling

Once you have that overall structure, there are various considerations for the specific creative. Introductory, social media lifestyle videos do very well. The first time you introduce yourself to a new customer, you want to tell your brand's story. What is your *why*, the reason at the heart of the company that would make a customer want you? This is a softer pitch than offering a download or an industry study, and it sets people up to like your company and think about doing business with you in the future.

For example, MUD\WTR ("mud water"), a coffee alternative, has an initial ad that provides a great case study of an introductory lifestyle approach. The company's founder, Shane Heath, used to be a creative director, and the ad shows his entire journey—starting the company, finding all the best ingredients, and bringing everything together as part of a lifestyle. He's working out, and he's striving to make the best product out there. Inside of that same ad, he positions MUD\WTR as a superior alternative coffee—one that contains one-seventh the caffeine, as well as some other basic stimulants derived from mushrooms. Unlike coffee, you can have it at any time of the day.

The ad tells a story about the product and why using it represents a better daily choice for yourself. Then, it explains Heath's mission: to take a chunk out of the coffee market. This long-form, top-of-funnel ad is highly engaging with high production quality. More importantly, it positions the product as part of a lifestyle, helping like-minded buyers begin to identify with the brand and what it's all about.

Further down the funnel, MUD\WTR ads are more micro-clips that nurture people through the process—each with specific offers and calls to action. By deferring those CTAs until later in the funnel, MUD\WTR puts a value on another essential fact of advertising: your buyers are normal human beings—and human beings don't like being sold to out of the gate. Start with storytelling, move into soft offers, and then make harder offers as your buyers move further along in the process. Once a person converts, the strategy becomes a matter of database management.

GOING DEEPER ON THE MOST EFFECTIVE AD TYPES

There are a few main ad formats that are effective online:

- **Company story videos.** Just like in the MUD\ WTR example, these tend to be top-of-funnel. Storytelling is at the heart of all effective marketing. When you lead with a direct conversion, you get very low click-through and engagement rates, and you never generate an emotional connection with the brand. So, it's essential to take the time to storyboard out exactly what the company story will look like, including the emotional resonance with customers. Generating a story is a process of identifying the *why* behind the company and ensuring that reason speaks to the customer's pain point. Then, turn the story into great video, photo, or text assets; use it at the top of the funnel in the first introduction, and make sure it gets in front of people.

- **Problem-and-solution ads.** While marketers often reserve these for further down the funnel, they are versatile and can be deployed anywhere after you've established your story. Sometimes they work well to create awareness, especially in industries where potential consumers don't even realize the problem exists. In those cases, generating awareness of the problem and immediately offering the solution can drive quite a bit of demand.

- **General offer.** People often don't take the time to think through the product they're advertising. It's important to compare exactly what you're offering to the options offered by your competitors. For example, say you're selling an e-course for $99 on how to train your dog, and your competitor is also selling a course on that topic for $120; their offer might be better than yours. You could improve your offer through additions such as access to a Facebook group, one live call with an expert dog trainer, a twenty-page PDF download checklist for dog training, 20 percent off any dog products on your website, or a free dog toy. Now, your offer would not just be a comparable course, but something much stronger. Always look at your price versus your competitors' price and then structure your ads to make it extremely clear that you have many substantive components with real value.

- **Direct call-to-action ads.** Usually, these direct appeals come at the bottom of the funnel. After someone has been in your audience for a sixty- to ninety-day period, seen your story, understood your general offer, been exposed to micro-conversions, and attended or been invited to an event, your best option is consistent, direct call-to-action ads. They typically take the form of a discount with a deadline, such as 30 percent off by March 30. When that deadline expires, you come out with a new discount and deadline. Keep repeating until it no longer makes sense and you cycle out the remaining audience.

- **Organic high-performing content on social media.** One emerging trend is the use of videos, photos, and text that perform well organically on social media— what may have started as something personal or motivational you posted on TikTok, Instagram, or LinkedIn, for instance—and making it your actual ad. Moving the organic high-performers over to the advertising side, you might add a soft call to action relating to your business. The strategy works well for a few reasons: (1) the content has proven to generate a strong organic reach, so it will get more exposure via the site algorithms; (2) people enjoy the content, so you have a better chance of converting at the end; and (3) even if they don't convert based on this particular ad, their enjoyment of watching it makes them more likely to see your next ad, too. Fun social creative in the upper funnel can pay off in the long run.

The exact order and approach of how you deploy your creative assets will depend on the push and pull between awareness and demand. For instance, if you sell bulk T-shirts online, most buyers don't care too much about the brand; they're just looking for the best price. In those cases, you might lead with specific ads around the value and then work on brand connotation later. In other cases, like with MUD\ WTR, few people are searching for cacao drinks and coffee alternatives, so the company needs to create awareness before making offers. Thus, in these two scenarios, you see the difference between a demand fulfillment strategy and an awareness strategy.

Testing Your Media Mix

Even though video is currently one of the most popular forms of media, it definitely shouldn't be the only aspect of your ad creative. It's a good idea to have a mix of different types of creative content, such as photos, animations, slideshows, and even direct copy.

If you're not sure what other kinds of ad creative to run, test it. Testing allows you to see what generates the best response from your audience, helping you to answer the key question of how to get real reach on each platform.

In addition to your ad creative, test your copy messaging as well. That way, you can determine not only the best kinds of creative content, but also the best copy to accompany it. The most successful combinations will gain natural traction. When they do, learn from their success and produce additional, similar content and make it even better.

If the ads don't perform well and the algorithms don't like them, they won't get you the exposure necessary to drive sales. That's why it's so important to make good ads that run well on the platform for which you designed them. In the age of machine learning and algorithms, creative that performs well on a platform is critical.

Pulling It All Together

A successful strategy comes down to your bidding and budgets working in tandem, the creative and copy assets you make, the specific placements, and then the frequency and engagement metrics (that is all before they hit your landing page!). Frequency is hugely important, because if you serve someone too many top-funnel or bottom-funnel ads, they'll eventually block you, and you'll lose access to that customer for life. The frequency needs to be consistent but not too annoying, so people are aware of your brand and view it positively. Generally, if you're showing an ad more than once every couple of days, it's too much.

CREATIVE TESTING

Often, brands run ads that perform fine, and then they simply turn the budget up or down. That's a mistake. Many organizations have been running the same ads since someone first set up the account, four or more years ago. That is a mistake, too. The ads might be doing okay, but they could be doing better with a systematic, iterative approach. They'll get much better results by constantly creating better ads and refining their audiences.

Without a testing framework, you're probably wasting 30 to 40 percent of your budget: your creative isn't optimized, and you're not penetrating your audiences as well as you could be. Meanwhile, your competitors who *are* testing will have a competitive advantage over you. The creative, the offer, and the messaging are all important.

In this section, I will outline a series of testing best practices to help you run a more efficient and effective program. Please note that there's a level of granularity and rigor to this approach that requires effort and skill. Not all organizations have the resources and staffing consistency to maintain these practices, which is why many brands outsource this work to a third-party provider.

Challenge the Winner

I'm going to describe example frameworks now that work for most ad platforms, such as Facebook, YouTube, and LinkedIn. Keep in mind, however, that some ad units are dynamic and don't allow for this exact approach. The framework still applies for these dynamic networks, but those networks will need to be updated differently. This section will help you understand the basic concept and how to apply it. Let's dive in.

Always have a minimum of five ads running at any given time. Determine your top two (or three). Then create three variations for each of those five ads, and test the variations against your winners.

These variations don't need to be big (but they can be). One might be a copy change. One might be an image change. One might be a video change. Make your change and run new tests on a monthly basis.

The next month, phase out the two ads performing the worst, continue with the three best performers, and then run new tests with two new challengers. Keep phasing out the ineffective and increasing the effective using this systematic approach.

Refresh Regularly

Plan to refresh your ad creative overall on at least an annual but preferably a quarterly basis. For instance, you could update the look and feel of your creative with a new photoshoot or video shoot. Keep repeating this process of testing the evergreen and refreshing creative at least twice—if not four times—a year. At Ignite Visibility, we offer a monthly creative refresh service for clients. We find this to be very effective, as each month their creative improves.

Monthly Tests

Plan to test a new audience every month. For instance, if you've run a normal in-market Google ad, try a test with audiences who have an income status over a certain threshold, who live in a certain state, who love watching movies or playing cricket, or who have some other potentially relevant characteristic with regard to your product. This test does not need to be a guess. As part of your regular program review, you should be looking at Google Analytics audiences and determining the lowest converters. I'll get more into this in a second.

It's best to test those audiences in a silo. If you're spending $100,000 a month, for instance, designate at least 10 percent of that budget ($10,000) for consistent monthly micro-testing to see if you can get a better CPA, ROAS, or customer LTV. Merge that data into the overall program, continuing to expand what works until you reach the metrics you're targeting. If a test performs better than your majority audience portfolio, then you know how to shift your ad monetization moving forward. It's an iterative process of refreshing, testing, and refining.

Make sure you have enough budget for your test. If you are running a test in Google Video Actions, Performance Max, YouTube, Facebook, etc.—anything algorithmic that needs flight and testing time and machine learning to self-improve— you need a budget of $500 to $1,000 a day minimum. That is the truth. Google says you should not even use their machine learning platforms unless you can commit to $500 a day for sixty to ninety days. While I understand you may be skeptical of this, as I was, I've seen it work, and it is really amazing to see the signals kick in and the sales take off.

Test New Audiences

When testing new audiences, many people fail to use Google Analytics to identify their highest converters and create a profile. Google Analytics allows you to filter by highest converters and see where they live, their age, their gender, which devices they're on, which devices they convert most on, and their affinity categories, such as baseball or movies. You can use that data to develop or expand your audience for paid media. Most people don't take the time to mine all that great historical data to create an audience in the ad system. This is a big mistake. Google Analytics connects it all together. Tell your team to review it!

But instead, many create an audience more haphazardly and wonder why it didn't convert. They look only at the platform analytics they run the ads in. This gives false positives on conversions and metrics. I can't tell you how many times I've seen paid media managers think they are doing well and reporting out-of-this-world positive conversion data. But they are really reporting on something that is not a qualified sale or lead. As mentioned earlier, you need MQL, SQL, and e-commerce sales data. Ensure your team shows you the *real* business value.

As you expand your paid media and digital marketing, you'll have more success if you can carry over the same characteristics from your top converters in Google Analytics.

Let me say this one more time, because far too people don't hear me whenever I bring this up. Look at the characteristics, each month, from the highest-converting users in Google Analytics, and use that for your native ad network targeting. This is a game-changer.

There's no sense in starting from scratch. Hit the ground running and then gather more data from there. You can build an avatar not just based on guessing but based on extremely specific data from Google Analytics.

I often see advertisers try to build avatars based on interviewing customers, talking to salespeople, conducting customer surveys, or hiring third-party companies. In my experience, those tactics are helpful for ad creative but can be a slow process. If you're new to market, you won't have any data, so start by reverse engineering competitors and the highest-performing products in the market, using the analytics and ad research tools that we mentioned earlier. Start with a small but meaningful budget, get proof of concept, and scale from there.

If you're *not* new to market, start with the characteristics of the highest converters on the website. All the data is there—why not look at the people who actually converted and made purchases to create your avatar, and figure out what would work the best with those people? It's a great trick of the trade that more advertisers should employ.

By looking at your conversion data, you might realize instead of running a national paid media campaign, it would be most effective to put 80 percent of the budget toward people who live in Texas and are in the top 30 percent economically. You're targeting a smaller audience, but they're more likely to respond.

New advertisers almost always start nationally. What a mistake! I was looking at a national campaign recently. They had a 3 percent conversion rate or better in most states, but in five states, they had a less than 1 percent conversion rate.

I asked them, "Do you care about these states?"

"Absolutely not," they said.

"If I could double your sales, would you be okay with me focusing your budget on just your top ten highest-converting states?" I asked.

What do you think they said in response?

"Heck yeah!"

In their case, I knew we could more than double their conversion rate. See, they could make ads, lists, and landing pages specific to their Google Analytics' highest-converting audience and state that they are running ads in. They could then scale their spend, increase sales, and use profits to invest in targeted city-level ads in those top states. (People in Beverly Hills and people in Bakersfield like to click on different types of creative, you know?) The key is to never stop. Have a culture of always improving. It's a mentality of always pushing and following the data. Most people get lazy and complacent when they hit targets. Never be happy... well, when it comes to ads at least.

QUALITIES OF EFFECTIVE CREATIVE

Good creative hooks people and catches their attention with something different. It doesn't just say "buy this now." It's amazing to see one ad that's so good, it can literally flip a crowded industry on its head and give more seasoned competitors a run for their money—like Dollar Shave Club and Manscaped did in the men's shaving industry. One great product can be scaled to the moon through a simple, clear offer. I love to see disruptors come in with laser precision—and the customer response to those standouts is pretty fun to watch, too. Just think, one good ad and offer is all you need!

Good creative makes it crystal clear how you're different, what your value is, and whether you're a current mainstream-er or an up-and-comer. Your product needs to look shiny, cut through the noise, and offer a better value proposition than the competition. Online sales often come from impulse buying, especially for a new product in an older category. So, your ad always needs to have a fresh look, highlight key differentiators, and feel like a deal.

Here's a tip: don't come online acting like you're better than all the other savvy digital-first businesses out there. You'll feel pain and lose money and then eventually realize you should have listened to your agency. I know that sounds blunt, but wouldn't you rather read that in this book than lose hundreds of thousands of dollars? Imagine if you just did all the stuff I explained in this book, as opposed to bringing a different approach online based on your past marketing experiences. The system in this book has been developed over twenty years, has worked for thousands of businesses, and has resulted in some of the best-run and most profitable campaigns online. What I am saying is: follow the program and don't try to make your own.

You need a mix of high-quality production that looks good. Then, mix in pieces that show real customers and influencers actually using and enjoying the product. Show people who the consumers would identify with and get them talking about the product's benefits and how it changed their life or addressed their problem.

The audience who will see the ad also dictates the creative. If the product centers on a well-known figure or celebrity, or if the ad will appear on their feed, then that person should be in the content, for instance. Do your homework and be careful with each consideration. Don't skip a step. Continually test and refine the tried-and-true approaches like stories, customer testimonials, offers, specials, and problem-solution ads, which are the best performers we see.

ACTION ITEMS

- Understand the sales funnel and consider which types of creative you will run at each stage of the customer's journey.

- Create a customer's journey map so that you can better understand your ideal customer and how to reach them.

- Develop your creative, emphasizing the concept, the copy, and the story.

- Audit the age of your current ads and set aside budget for refreshing and testing new creative.

CHAPTER 8

DATABASE MANAGEMENT

t is very common for new customers to message me on
LinkedIn. Here is a story about one who reached out who
was just plain frustrated.

They'd been in the industry for fifteen years and had
controlled the space for most of that time. Recently, however, competitors who had only been in the market for less
than a year were suddenly eating their lunch. Shouldn't the
fifteen-year veteran have the advantage, with many more
customers and a bigger database? They asked me this question and, well, I agreed.

I could tell something was wrong. I thought to myself, *They must not have a good data management program*. That is usually the case in this sort of scenario. An older business just wins for so long and they often get disorganized and complacent.

In order to get back ahead of their competitors, we decided to revamp their paid media strategy. This involved a database clean-up and segmentation—starting with their email list. As we discovered, they had a decent-sized list of about 25,000 people. However, only about 1,000 were active customers. Of the remaining 24,000 names, about 30 percent had been customers in the past, while the other half had entered their information but never converted. Both the past customers and the ones who never became customers represented excellent opportunities. As is standard procedure, we needed to take the non-converters and push them over the edge, and then take the past customers and run a win-back campaign.

From there, we subdivided these contacts into groups based on the last time they interacted with an email in the last three, six, or twelve months. We also looked at how they'd made contact—was it through an event, a lead form, a guide, or a newsletter pop-up? We found people who had reached out through the lead form were the highest-quality prospects, followed by event attendees, followed by the guide, and finally the newsletter leads.

Using that information, we set up a series of ads to target the most promising subgroups. In addition, we created similar and lookalike audiences on Google and Facebook based on the people who had used the lead form.[18]

18 If you don't know how that works, Google and Facebook will take a list, analyze the qualities of the people, and find people like them within a percentage of range designated. For example, you could do a 1 percent or 5 percent look-alike audience.

We filtered the lookalike groups to only those people inside the United States and then used what's called bid adjustment to spend more on the top markets based on our Google Analytics data. We also captured data from people who filled out the form but didn't convert, targeting them with emails and text messages to get them to return.

This effort, along with coordinated email marketing, resulted in taking the company from a 20 percent growth rate year over year to well over 80 percent. They went on to have two record quarters, and, as of this writing, we are still running the campaigns.

This is an example of what's possible with good database management. There's a lot of out there, but you have to dig and know what you're looking for. If you take the time to identify and capture the data, you can maximize customer LTV.

Every business has data, but they often manage it poorly and lack foresight, education, and organization skills. Newer businesses especially tend to do an extremely poor job with data, if they even consider it. The bigger the company gets, the more important database management becomes.

At a minimum, organizations should invest in a CRM—and dedicate the time necessary to capture and sort detailed, accurate data sets. This isn't just a good idea. In many ways, data is the primary engine for growing your business and maximizing customer LTV. Maximizing customer LTV is the focus of sophisticated and mature businesses. The more customers a business has had, the more opportunities they have to move forward.

Database management represents the foundation of all future digital marketing—especially in a cookieless future. As cookies go away and ad platforms gather less data and have fewer automatic opt-ins, it will be more important than ever for businesses to maintain good databases to target offers and get people into the funnel.

In this chapter, we'll explore the basics of effective database management. It's important to understand that with cookies going away and privacy becoming increasingly regulated, both first-party data (data you own and have the rights to utilize) and third-party data (data someone else owns and has the rights to utilize, but you legally contract to access) are increasingly important. Database management represents your greatest asset to achieve a competitive advantage in both digital marketing and businesses in general. If you don't attend to these issues now, you'll regret it later. If your database is a mess, it's essential to either clean it up yourself or hire someone to clean it up for you.

TAGGING DATA AND LEAD SCORING

Clients come to us with goals like "10,000 leads a month" or "$5 million in e-commerce sales in a month." In general, most have a number in mind, but they don't always think about important quality metrics.

When you're forecasting, it's important to think of lead quality. Not all customers have the same LTV. Ten thousand leads might sound like a lot, for instance, but if only half of them are any good, then you need to know which ones.

Database management allows you to differentiate your

high-value and low-value leads. To do this, you must be able to tag data. How did the data come in? Was it from a specific landing page, call to action, webinar, a pop-up email capture on the website, a lead form, or a white paper download?

It's important to assign a score to whatever method brought the data into the system. Scoring systems vary. Most people use a scale from one to five. Those scores give you the ability to figure out how much energy you should spend on following up with the customer and how (e.g., phone, email, other targeted marketing). Whatever you capture here—and however you score your leads—will inform your marketing approach through all other channels as you nurture prospective customers further down the funnel. In other words, don't skip it.

USEFUL DATABASE TOOLS

Many businesses make the big mistake of continually buying new database management tools. They think they need a particular feature that their current tools don't have, and before they know it, they're paying for a host of subscriptions that don't integrate with each other. Businesses around the globe suffer from "shiny object syndrome," buying the next hot thing and not actually being able to work with any of their data in a meaningful way.

There are many different systems out there, so before you start with database tools and pick your software, sit down with a professional or do your research to figure out exactly what you need and how you'll put it together. Decide which system you'll use for each of the following needs:

- CRM to hold all the information about your customers

- Project management

- Time-tracking within the company

- Invoicing, including consideration of how a payment will connect to your bank account and financial statements

- Human resources

- Customer surveys

- Marketing technology

- Sales

- Data visualization

- Forecasting

- Email

- File sharing

- Security

- Internal messaging

I understand some of the categories mentioned above are outside of marketing, but you would be surprised how they overlap.

Map out your needs before you start and figure out the core and secondary systems by department. Popular systems include Microsoft Suite, Google Workspace, Marketo, Salesforce, Tableau, HubSpot, Segment, Clearbit, Snowflake, and BigQuery. There are so many marketing tools. The right choice for each function depends on what you're looking for, which is why you need to determine your needs in advance.

From a marketing and customer management perspective, try to do as much as you can in one platform before attempting to integrate with another. Management gets messy when datasets exist in different databases. Do everything possible to avoid the need for integrations, and just work within your core CRM.

MAPPING DATA TO OFFERS

With effective database management, marketers have the ability to determine where a lead has originated and how best to follow up. They can also establish first-part data-building plans before a product's launch or a customer event, or before leads even need to be generated. Here are a few examples.

Targeted Offers

Imagine you host workshops on how to be the best real estate agent in California and you want to build a database of real estate professionals to sell the workshop when it's time to promote. You might run an ad with a guide on how home prices will change in the state over the next five years. You'll then have this first-party data ready to run ads to and send email blasts, as well as call, when it's time to promote.

Promoting New Events

Say you've done ten different webinars over the years, with 500 people per webinar. You have all their data—and 5,000 email addresses that you know are in your target audience. Now that you have another webinar coming up, those 5,000 prior attendees would be a great audience to receive an email blast invite for your new event.

Creating Lookalike Audiences

Data is great because it builds on itself over time. Looking back at our previous example, you could also take those 5,000 email addresses, upload them to an ad platform, and then create a lookalike audience based on the percentage of similarity you want between the new audience and the source audience. Then, you can use the existing data to find people who have those similar characteristics and advertise to them.

You can also overlay the lookalike audience with the characteristics from the Google Analytics conversion metrics, such as age, income, location, and so on. Or, for instance, you could create subgroups in your database, such as people who attended a webinar, those who downloaded a certain offer, or people who found you organically and signed up for your highest-ticket item.

DATABASE NURTURING

It's generally good to have (introductory) low-ticket, mid-ticket, and high-ticket offers. Many businesses will start with a low-ticket offer—maybe the product (or service) is just a dollar, which just gets the customer to commit to something. Down the road, the business will sell them higher-ticket items.

In a digital marketing mastermind group that I'm in, they

call this a *tripwire*. A tripwire means offering something online with a ton of value for very cheap to gain a customer's data and to get them comfortable with putting their card down and having it on file with you. Next, you sell them multiple products as part of the offer bump process. A bump offer is when you try to get a customer to bump up their offer or add something additional to their cart.

There are a few other concepts that are important to know here:

- **Upsells.** This is when you have another price presented for a larger and better offer.

- **Downsells.** This is when someone is going to abandon an offer so you present them with a less expensive offer.

- **Post-conversion calls to action.** Basically, after you make a sale or get a conversion, a post-conversion call to action means you try to sell them a special offer on a thank-you page.

Let's talk a little more about monetizing data and backend offers, just so you're aware of what is possible.

Say you do lead generation in the loan space. You run an ad for a guide to getting the least expensive loan for the most money going into the next year. Someone comes in and fills out that form. Now, their data has been captured. You know this person is interested in getting a loan. Now, note there are probably twenty other similar companies that offer similar services and are interested in that same lead.

You don't necessarily need to get the lead on the phone and offer them a loan for this lead to be valuable; it might make sense to sell the data to different service providers for a fee or a percentage of the sale. The lead's value could compound as different sellers monetize the data and as the customer gets further and further down the funnel.

Another example might be someone selling a real estate book... who also wants to sell the same customer a ticket to a real estate event, real estate coaching sessions, a real estate mastermind group, an "I'm the best realtor in the world" T-shirt, and/or a real estate champion teddy bear. The point is, it's important to understand how to maximize the value of a customer within an LTV process that makes sense in the context of your business, while doing so in a way that is fully legal and aboveboard. This can happen all in your own business or through monetization partners. I'm not necessarily endorsing strictly data sales, and it's not something that I practice, but it's an option to be aware of. I do practice customer LTV mapping and have referral partners in some of my businesses. It is all professional and by the book.

KPIS

Here is where forecasting and data come into play in sophisticated organizations. Sophisticated organizations understand how many new customers are coming in, when to close a customer, the organization's close rate and churn rate, their business's overall revenue net income, what they need to do in order to fill the funnel, and more. They systematically work to improve those metrics so that they lose less and can scale the business over time.

They also have well-developed win-back programs, which

is a process to bring back old customers through digital marketing. This is why we stressed the importance of determining your goals and KPIs as you first worked to set up your marketing program.

For instance, say you want to grow by 40 percent this year. Currently, you bring in $300,000 in new sales from 300 new customers a month. To hit your target, you not only need to grow the sales from your current customers, but you'll need to grow sales from those 300 customers by 40 percent as well. The digital marketing plan unfolds from that target, based on the close rate and lead scoring. To then set and hit these KPIs, you need the big picture, rooted in accurate data.

VISUALIZING REVENUE BY PRODUCT LINE

Once organizations set up a robust, accurate database, they can create a visualization of contribution margin, revenue, gross profit, and net income by product line, which, believe it or not, can also tie into the ad system on some level. That visualization allows you to determine which lines are best for business and design your ad strategy accordingly. You'll know how much a product generates in revenue on a monthly basis, what the churn rate is, and what marketing you need to feed into that product. Each line becomes a micro-business model. You can then level up to multiple products in a category and then to the overall business.

Google Ads offers gross profit from units sold, gross profit margin, lead gross profit from units sold, lead gross profit margin column, and more. According to Google,

> *Search Ads 360 can compute a rough measure of the profits you earn from each transaction. To do this, you'll need to update your Merchant Center feed with information about your cost for each of the products that you sell. Search Ads 360 will subtract the total cost from each of the products listed in a transaction from the total revenue from those same products.*[19]

An ad account is really a business in itself: the revenue per ad, per ad group, and the whole campaign tells a clear story. If you can match your database to the ad account, you have an edge. Almost all CRMs will allow you to create this type of visualization, and if they can't, there is a third-party tool or custom integration to make it happen. In Salesforce, for example, for a business services company, you can associate revenue to anything that you want and then build a systematic process around that data. You should also be able to sort by customer type.

KEEP IT CLEAN

Keep your databases organized and as simple as possible. Often, clients have messy databases they can't use, and they regret not getting on top of their data sooner. Investing in fixes now is better than missing out on opportunities later. Database management and cleanup are iterative processes; attend to them early and often.

---

19   "Report on Purchase Details: Enable Reporting on Profit," Search Ads 360 Help, accessed August 2, 2022, https://support.google.com/searchads/answer/6089052?hl=en.

ACTION ITEMS

- Determine the sources of your leads and which are the highest value.

- Dedicate at least twenty hours per month to refining, segmenting, and scoring your database until it's 100 percent clean and functional.

- Once your data is clean and organized, automate.

CHAPTER 9

AD AND AUDIENCE OPTIMIZATION

P rocesses are important. In this chapter, I'll teach you why. Someone I know made a big mistake once. Instead of entering $30,000 per month in an ad spend field, they accidentally entered $30,000 per *day*—and they had no process in place to catch the mistake.

The erroneous budget ran for four days before someone else noticed the error. By that time, the company had spent

$100,000 over their budget—wiping out the next month's worth of budget in the process.

This kind of nightmare scenario should never happen. And yet, the failure to check basic metrics like daily spending and pacing is one of the biggest, most common mistakes in all of paid media. Sometimes, like my client, organizations will lose money to overspending. Other times, they lose opportunities by underspending.

Either mistake is costly. If you need 10,000 leads a month to hit your goals, for instance, but for some reason the ad platform only spends half or a quarter of your budget, it can impact the entire company. Without enough leads coming in, revenue may drop, forcing you to lay off people. So, it's essential to attend to these issues in the right sequence and timeframe.

Fortunately, while errors like this may be all too common, they can be stopped. In fact, with the right checks and balances in place, they're highly preventable.

A good digital marketer knows exactly how to structure their time and maintain good account hygiene. They know what tasks require weekly, monthly, quarterly, or annual maintenance. This all may sound a little perfunctory, but it can mean a difference in millions of dollars of revenue for your business.

Whether you're a leader, a team member, or a consultant, this chapter is essential reading for maintaining the health of your digital marketing program. With a clear and consistent schedule, you can easily avoid costly mistakes. In this chapter, I have provided a comprehensive checklist of what a good ad and audience optimization program should look like, so you can hand it to your team and ask if they're checking all these boxes. Or, you can do it yourself. While every company's process will vary, this is a pretty great general framework from which to start, if I do say so myself.

YOUR OPTIMIZATION PROGRAM

Here's what you or your digital media manager should be attending to daily, weekly, and monthly to stay on track.

Daily

CHECK THE PACING

Create a dashboard so that every morning when you have your coffee, you can log in and make sure you're getting the desired number of leads or sales coming in to allow you to hit your goal for the month.

VERIFY YOUR SPENDING

Sometimes, ad systems allow for budget variability, leading to spending more than you want on a campaign. During the daily check, make sure you're not spending more or less than intended during your review so you know when to adjust.

REVIEW ACCOUNT PERFORMANCE

As you get further into the day, you'll also want to review your account performance week over week, month over month, and year over year, to see how you're trending. Check the following to make sure everything is moving in the right direction:

- Conversion volume
- Cost per acquisition (CPA)
- Conversion rate
- Ad spend
- CTR
- Average CPA
- CPM

Also, check all of the most important elements for each account. If something is off, such as a low conversion rate or volume, make changes accordingly.

CHECK YOUR METRICS

This is perhaps the most important daily task. Having a systematic approach for each paid media site ensures everything gets handled correctly and nothing veers too far off course. You're like a pilot in a plane, making sure all the gauges look good.

SET UP FOR THE NEXT DAY

Toward the end of the day, set up your campaign launches and creative swaps for the next day.

Weekly

CHECK YOUR REPORTING

Follow up on anything that didn't go as planned during the week.

REVIEW YOUR AUTO-APPLY RECOMMENDATIONS

It's important to note that auto-apply recommendations will automatically make changes for you—without your approval—if that's how you have set it. Here, it's important to distinguish between a *recommendation* engine and an *auto-apply* engine. An auto-apply engine will automatically put in certain rules for you—such as a negative keyword list across campaigns—and then *act* on those.

All the big ad systems now include this relatively new feature, which uses machine learning to find areas for account improvement.

EXAMINE YOUR CHANGE HISTORY

Make sure that any changes made are in line with the plan and no one has altered anything incorrectly or made a mistake.

CHECK THE OVERALL HYGIENE OF THE ACCOUNT

Look at your audience reporting, remove any keywords that don't have traffic, take out negative keywords that shouldn't be there or you don't want to run ads on, and remove any keywords that are duplicates.

Make sure you have plenty of traffic going to all your different ads in the system. Review your data-driven attribution. Are your conversions being tracked and applied correctly to machine learning, bidding, and so on? Optimizations, bids, and budgets should also be reviewed weekly.

OTHER IMPORTANT ACTIONS

Here are the other essential weekly tasks:

- Validate your testing
- Run experiments
- Measure, analyze, and set objectives
- Find and leverage any new data that comes in to improve the campaigns

As you see what's working and what's not, you want to develop new hypotheses and create variations of tests to implement for your ads, copy, landing pages, segmentation, targeting, and the different bidding models you're using.

Monthly

WEEK ONE

During the first week of each month, conduct a review of the prior month's performance. What went well, and what didn't? Start the month with a set of priorities for what you'll do to drive improvement. Update your spending and pacing as well as your media plan. Which new ads are you launching? What's your budget? Are you trying any new networks?

WEEK TWO

Focus on targeting and messaging. What ad copy will you use, and which variations will you test?

WEEK THREE

This is a great time to examine your competition. What are your competitors doing within all the different ad platforms? What types of ads are they launching? What are their budgets?

WEEK FOUR

Use everything you've learned to plan for the next month. What can you take from your analysis of competitors and current campaigns to inform actions regarding your campaign structure, bidding strategies, different settings, keyword mapping, and A/B tests?

Next, identify growth opportunities for the coming month. Should you expand into networks like YouTube, display, or programmatic? Should you try enhanced conversions, value-based bidding, or Performance Max? Should you add any new audiences?

Continually allocate 10 percent of your budget toward new growth opportunities, particularly when an established network becomes too expensive or you've reached a saturation point. Some networks perform better than others. Search networks generally perform the best because they have the highest intent—people are searching for products to address their issues. Paid media follows.

The overarching question is whether you can get conversions more cheaply on another network, so you always want to be testing. With the right model, you can get the most conversions for the least cost on each network and know what the highest profitability would be for each network. Start with a test budget around 10 percent of ad spend for a network to get good data, allowing you to build from there.

Plan for the Future

In addition to performing their daily, weekly, monthly, and yearly hygiene, skilled digital marketers always have one eye to the future so they can understand emerging trends and adapt their practices.

From our vantage point at Ignite Visibility, there are currently three key market trends for the agency ecosystem:

1. **Measurement:** As the customer's journey becomes increasingly complex, businesses will need more data and a better understanding of that data across all channels than ever before. One of the biggest opportunities is improving data visualization and tracking. Measurement will be critical, and businesses that don't put in the time to invest in setting up measurement tools will miss out on the benefits.

2. **Automation:** Without measurement, you also can't take advantage of automation. All of the new ad platforms are working on automating advertising so that users can focus on higher-level decisions without the need for so much manual adjustment. Automation requires accurate conversion data to help machine learning perform better over time. According to a 2020 Google study, 93 percent of brands see automation as a valuable or critical part of working with

agencies and their marketing teams over the next three years.[20]

3. **Display and video:** There's more display inventory available than businesses can take advantage of, even as the web grows more competitive with regard to search and paid social. Using this seemingly endless supply requires accurate measurement and data-driven automation. With those pieces in place, you can use Google to find people similar to converters and target them accordingly. We recommend doing so through video-based ads. Platforms want to push videos because they garner more engagement than still images. People look at a still image for a second, but they will watch a video for minutes. Social sites want to increase a user's overall "dwell time."

Because of the agency's market trends, the way that paid media and digital marketing people do their jobs is shifting dramatically. In the past, these marketers were involved in campaign management and continually tweaking various aspects. With the rise of automation, that hands-on involvement will decrease. Instead, there will be much more emphasis on creative auditing, development, marketing strategy, advanced data analytics, and insights. There will also be a need for better integration with different marketing technology stacks, understanding of how different types of marketing technology help paid media, and focus on attribution and advanced measures.

20 Forrester and Google, Reclaim Growth with Rapid Agency Transformation: Agencies that Transform Capabilities and Master Technology to Drive Customer-First Strategies Will Succeed in Delivering On Brands' Urgent Growth Imperative, Forrester Consulting Thought Leadership Paper, July 2020, https://services.google.com/fh/files/emails/forrester_research_paper.pdf.

Each of the different ad platforms will score you on how well you've optimized, and you should strive to improve that score. Set up all of your tagging and tracking correctly. Take advantage of the auto-applied recommendations, offline conversion tracking, and enhanced conversions, as well as conversion-based, smart, and value-based bidding.

Digital marketing will continue to move in the direction of optimizing toward the endgame of customer LTV. Yes, CPA, cost for acquisition, cost of sales, ROAS, and profit are good, but the ad systems ultimately drive toward using customer LTV to inform all of your bidding.

In the future, we'll also see all marketing channels breaking down into one of three objectives: growing online sales, generating leads, or growing in-store sales. Each ad platform will create their different services around those options.

Get Organized

If you want to optimize, don't be sloppy. Be highly detailed in the way that you capture and organize all of your customers' data. You want your customers' data to feel like a perfect library or a project initiated by the military—perfectly organized. It should be maximally organized, stored over time, and tagged by quality and category. Your customers' data is your biggest asset.

If you take the time to set up your tracking and measurement in an organized way, you'll be able to take advantage of all of the new ways to advertise online. People who optimize will have much more success over the next five to ten years than those who try to run cold traffic, which simply won't work as well as it used to. The new digital landscape represents a major opportunity for legacy businesses that have organized correctly, as well as new businesses that stay on top of these issues from the beginning.

From what I've seen, only about 10 percent of businesses currently have these processes set up correctly. By 2025, I estimate that number will rise to 70 percent, driven by the shift away from using cookies.

Following the guidance here can multiply your traffic and conversions. For example, one of my clients, a lawyer, worked with us to set up enhanced conversions, machine learning, and data-driven attribution. He was originally running $10,000 a month in ad spend and getting about 50 conversions per month as a result. Once we got him dialed in, he had the confidence to scale his spend to $30,000 per month, garnering him closer to 300 conversions per month, doubling his conversions per ad spend.

ACTION ITEMS

- Create a checklist for daily, weekly, monthly, quarterly, and yearly optimization tasks.

- Determine who on your team is accountable to these tasks.

- Dedicate regular time to keeping yourself current on future and emerging trends.

CONCLUSION

I worked with a major media company that ran its digital marketing on a whim. The team was more focused on the main business and brought us in to help with search engine optimization and digital strategy consulting.

Within the first week of working together, we discovered that a folder in a subdomain of the website had been hacked.

Here was a company spending hundreds of thousands of dollars per month on ads, not realizing they directed people to these bad pages. Had they practiced proper maintenance of the site, they could have caught the issue much earlier— and in the process, protected not only their own data, but their customers' as well.

The moral of the story is clear: take digital marketing seriously.

Digital marketing today is not like it was five years ago. It has turned into a giant, sophisticated business. Where once digital marketing merely required some minimal initiative to get clicks from a Google ad, today it has evolved to touch all aspects of a business. If this sounds like an exaggeration, it's not. Modern digital marketing now has major legal and financial implications. It can tie into your project management systems, customer data, and financials. It can play a role in and be impacted by your cybersecurity.

In this new, highly competitive environment, the leaders who succeed are the ones who run everything online with as much care as they run their businesses offline. Anything that goes into a great offline business—including knowing what your structures, processes, and timeframes look like—applies online. All of the useful frameworks you learn in business, from Lean Manufacturing and Six Sigma to books like *Winning* and *Traction*, apply to managing your digital marketing as well.

People who recognize its importance are investing in optimizing and advancing as a result, so you need to as well. The approaches I've outlined in this book will help you stay ahead of the curve.

As you set out on your digital marketing journey, let the lessons in this book be your guide. Revisit the legalities around digital marketing at least once a quarter to make sure you're up to date. Set up strong cybersecurity and a data management policy to protect your customers' data. Invest in the best video creative around and the best data-driven attribution so you can take advantage of opportunities like machine learning.

Finally, always be testing, trying new networks, and expanding the program. Make sure you're not too invested in one bucket, and you'll achieve success.

The frameworks covered in this book will help you stay on the cutting edge with your creative and paid media marketing management, putting you ahead of many of your competitors. But in order to do it, you need to do it right.

KEEP THE CONVERSATION GOING

If you enjoyed this book and would like to learn more, you can connect with us in one of the following ways:

- Check out my courses at johnlincoln.marketing.

- Check out my instructional videos on Ignite Visibility's YouTube channel.

- Check out Certainty Tech, our media mix forecasting software, which allows you to bring certainty to digital marketing.

- I would also love to connect with you online. You can find me on Twitter at @JohnELincoln.

ACKNOWLEDGMENTS

A great deal of effort went into creating this book. I would like to thank Evan Trevers from Google; Eythor Westman, Connor Brown, Meghan Parsons, and Mezar Chakwa from Ignite Visibility; and our agency team leads from Meta, Yelp, Microsoft, and other ad platforms who supplied data.

I would also like to thank our clients at Ignite Visibility, whom we challenge to push new boundaries in digital marketing every day, and who trust us to do so.

Finally, I'd like to thank my family for allowing me time to work on this book.

ABOUT THE AUTHOR

John Lincoln (MBA) is CEO of Ignite Visibility, a highly sought-after digital marketing strategist, keynote speaker, and winner of the coveted Search Engine Land "Search Marketer of the Year" award.

Ignite Visibility is a leading performance-marketing agency specializing in multichannel digital strategy, SEO, paid media, social media, creative, email, PR, Amazon, and CRO. Founded on the principles of relationships, responsiveness, and results, Ignite has been named the #1 SEO company, #1 Paid Media Company, #1 Social Media Company, and #1 Digital Agency in the United States. This success has propelled it to the 2017, 2018, 2019, 2020, 2021, and 2022 *Inc. 5000* list. Ignite Visibility has a proprietary, multi-channel, performance-based forecasting system and software allowing businesses to clearly hit goals.

His business's mission is to help others through digital marketing and use the profits to invest in his clients' success, employees' success, and in his community. With nearly twenty years of demanding experience, Lincoln has worked with over 1,000 online businesses. Through work with these, and many other clients, he has helped take hundreds of websites to the #1 position in Google for respective competitive keywords, built social communities into millions of followers, strategized many record-breaking advertising campaigns with millions in monthly spend, and worked on hundreds of advanced projects in CRO, influencer marketing, media buys, email, Amazon, and affiliate marketing.

Lincoln has authored thousands of articles and videos, including regular contributions to *Inc.* and *Entrepreneur*, as well as features in *Forbes*, *The New York Times*, and more. He has authored two books, "The Forecaster Method" (2019) and "Digital Influencer" (2016), and is the Producer and Director of "SEO: The Movie" and "Social Media Marketing: The Movie."

He has received the Most Admired CEO Award and Top Business Leaders Under 40 Award. He has spoken at conferences and events like Web Summit, SMX, and Pubcon, and has taught at UC San Diego since 2010.

Made in the USA
Las Vegas, NV
11 December 2022

61823523R00116